"The book is such a compelling read. Full of insights into how to lead a business through purpose, 'simple' human principles and relentless search for the new and never done before."

—Ale Bellini
Chief Customer Officer
Tesco

"Seeing how this volatile world we live in unfolds, reading this book it is evident to me how the principles John embedded into VIA are becoming every day not just more relevant but also very much needed if we want to improve the way we live our lives."

—Alberto Di Leo
Regional Vice President
Ice Cream Europe
Unilever

"John's philosophy on maintaining a set of principles while growing a company is a deeply wise and essential part of any leader's perspective."

—Michael Ventura
CEO
Sub Rosa

"The principles that John and VIA live by have helped Welch's discover new growth opportunities over many years."

—Brad Irwin
CEO
Welch's

"Coleman delivers a spirited set of principles in concise, candid, anecdotal form. I constantly reference this book, and its messages are enduring for a world in radical flux."

—John Melick
President
Blue Medium

"To know where you want to go in business you first need to know who you are, why you exist, your purpose—and define your success. John Coleman understands this, and he understands the need for sound principles/values as the core foundation and driving force for business and life. One of the best minds I've ever worked with and a great read for every leader."

—Todd Pendleton
Marketing visionary and former Global Brand Communications Director
Nike
and CMO
Samsung Telecommunications America

"John Coleman has become an extraordinary example of a leader who has succeeded by applying positive principles to life and business. His book VIA PRINCIPLES illustrates how readers can cultivate their own principles to discover the foundation for a positive and rewarding life."

—Scott Williams
President
The Nantucket Project

"VIA PRINCIPLES *provides tools for leadership and problem-solving; an essential book for anybody working to bring an organization to the next level.*"

—Katie Sonnenborn and Sarah Workneh
Co-Directors
Skowhegan School of Painting & Sculpture

"*This book shows how leaders can be successful by sticking to business principles that you can tell your mom about.*"

—Roger Bailey
Managing Director Process Industries
ABB

"*A timely and important reminder of the power of staying true to one's core values—in business and in life.*"

—Naomi McMahon
SVP, Head of Strategic Marketing & Partnerships
Universal Music Group

VIA PRINCIPLES

VIA PRINCIPLES
Finding Growth Through Creativity, Collaboration and Compassion

John R. Coleman

PORTLAND, MAINE

Publisher:
JRC, Inc.
26 Cushman St.
Portland, Maine 04102
jcoleman@theviaagency.com

© 2016, 2017 by John R. Coleman
All rights reserved.
First edition 2016. Second edition 2017.

ISBN: 978-0-9972640-1-2
Printed in the United States of America
Library of Congress Control Number: 2017935113

To Linda, the best collaborator I will ever have.

Contents

Introduction   xi

VIA Principles   1

1. Be Curious   5
   When in Doubt Always Ask Why   6
   Fearless Curiosity Sets Us Free   8
   Be a Hedonist of the Mind   10
   Purpose Unlocks Curiosity   11

2. Honor the Process   15
   The Liberation of Constraints   16
   Collaboration Stacks the Deck   19
   Conflict Is Not a Four-Letter Word—*Dick* Is   20
   These Things Just Don't Happen   22

3. Think Like the Audience   25
   Love Listening   26
   Go Live in the Wild   28
   Being the Same Is So Boring   29
   Sympathy Is Passive, Empathy Is Active, Compassion Is Transformative   32
   Caring Is an Amphetamine   34

4. Create Respect   37
   A Golden Rule   39
   No Gossip Is the Best Kind of Gossip   42
   There Are Many Views From the Ship We Sail   43
   Fighting for Respect   47

5. Be on Time   49
   Harnessing the Unstoppable   50
   Planning, Priorities and Patience   52
   Every Idea Has Its Time   55
   Take the Long View   57

6. Be on Budget   63
   Always Invest, Rarely Spend   64
   Know the Price of the Priceless   66
   Budgets Aren't Small, but Thinking Can Be   67
   Don't Be Fair, Be Overly Fair   68

7. Figure It Out   71
   Persistence, the Unsexy Cousin of Creativity, Rules   72
   Et Tu, Collaboration?   74
   Fact Over Fiction   76
   Fail Forward   78
   And Now for Something Completely Different ...   80

8. Find the Magic   83
   Let It Flow   85
   Screw Around More   88
   Our Ideas vs. My Ideas   90
   To Be or Not to Be   94
   A Case for Crafting Magical Work   97

CONTENTS

9. Do Work That Makes You Proud   99
    The World Should Be Like Gertrude Stein's
        Living Room   100
    Give Away All the Credit   102
    Always Better Your Best   103
    Can You Have Too Many Parties?   105
    Pride of Ownership   107

10. Believe   109
    Imagining a Better Way: Vision, Instinct, Action   110
    Act Like You Believe   113
    Pragmatic Optimism   116
    Dream an Impossible Dream   119

A Few Final Thoughts About Principles   123

Reflection and Discussion Guidelines   127

Acknowledgments   143

About the Author   145

Artwork: *Principles*   147

Colophon   149

x

Introduction:
In Search of a New Kind of Growth

*You need power only when you want to do something harmful.
Otherwise, love is enough to get everything done.*
—Charlie Chaplin

We are living in a time of great uncertainty. Technological, political, environmental and social changes are upending our systems and mores each day. It can seem overwhelming. But I feel there is enormous potential for growth ahead of us. To see this opportunity, perhaps we need to better define and understand what kinds of growth we might pursue. Not all growth is created equally. Too often growth is defined only in monetary terms—and I have come to believe, now more than ever, the old adage that money does not buy happiness. I believe we should be searching for a new kind of growth, one that enriches our experiences as humans without harming the people and world around us. This means the value of our growth needs to be measured not only monetarily but much more comprehensively, assessing it for its kindness, fairness, safety and sustainability (both human and environmental), and for the joy and awareness it brings about. These are not your typical criteria for success in our economy, but I think they should be. There is a lot more to this growth game—and for the sake of our collective future, we could all stand to get better at playing it.

This book explores the results of an experiment in capitalism I have been conducting since 1993 called The VIA Agency. VIA is an advertising agency I co-founded, and by trying to lead the agency with a focus on creativity, collaboration, caring and compassion while adhering to 10 guiding principles of operation, I think we have discovered a richer understanding of this new kind of growth. In this book, I share lessons I have learned and stories that bring those insights to life. To say we had everything figured out as a company would be terribly naïve and untrue, but by constantly striving to find better ways of doing everything in our day-to-day work, the net result of our growth has been as positive as possible.

I hope the book gives you many good ideas big and small to share. I initially wrote it for current and future employees of the agency, publishing it only for internal use in 2016. Then the world started changing rapidly. Now my intent for sharing this book publicly is to cultivate more dialogue about the role principles can play in strengthening a person's, an organization's or a community's positive impact on the world. By encouraging and prompting greater reflection on and exploration of our principles, we can set the stage for opportunities, ideas and ultimately actions that create healthier growth. I am not saying the specific principles in this book are the right and best ones for you or your organization to follow; I am saying that investigating, discovering and committing to a collection of positive principles that feel right for you or your organization will lead to new and much better growth.

There is one thing, however, that I believe emphatically: Any principle worth choosing to follow must have a "positive" nature.

INTRODUCTION

Positive principles must not favor some at the expense of others. Positive principles must not negate or diminish what is universally good. Positive principles must point to openness, tolerance and compassion, and away from fear, greed, ignorance and hate. No principles grounded in the "negative" have stood the test of time. All hope is grounded in optimism and collective goodness. This is the one statement in my book that I will respectfully defend with anyone: The world will prosper only when we celebrate and live by positive principles. My concern today is that we are heading away from this idea, so it is imperative to start a dialogue about positive principles now.

To this end, I have added a discussion guide at the end of the book to help aid in both personal reflection and group dialogue on the role of principles in your world. When reflecting on these questions and topics, I find it helpful to begin by contextualizing them for your specific situation. Each of us lives with different privileges and oppressions—to make for richer dialogue, these realities should be recognized to the best of the group's ability. By trying to hold everyone's unique circumstances in our minds, we stand a better chance of reaching true understanding and thus being able to evolve more constructively.

My real hope for this book is to have all who read it ask themselves if they are achieving the growth they desire in their own lives. I want us all to reflect on our personal principles and examine whether we are living by them daily. Are we open to the plights of others and how we can be of service to the world in ways that bring about inclusive, equitable and loving growth? I hope this book is an invitation to us all to find a better way. Let's not get stuck living someone else's definition of success. We can break the molds we see around us and stay open to the beauty of sharing and giving our all with others.

The secret lies in unearthing the principles that bring more kindness, equality and freedoms into our world. Let's find those principles and live by them. And may we all grow in ways never dreamed possible.

VIA PRINCIPLES
Finding Growth Through Creativity, Collaboration and Compassion

The week I began to write this book I lost a close friend and mentor, Kip Moore, who was also a longtime board member of VIA. He was a singular person and an invaluable adviser to me, plus a very successful venture capitalist and a wonderful human being in all walks of his life. But when it came to talking about himself, he was pretty reserved.

Still, when I was asked to write a eulogy for his service, I found it very easy because he was a person of such strong principles—humble, kind, lighthearted, frugal, curious, self-reliant and extraordinarily generous. I felt a deep understanding of him simply from having observed the clarity and consistency of his deeds.

I believe that people with a clear understanding of their own principles can live a more fulfilled and possibly happier life. It's not that they don't make mistakes—or that they're any better than anyone else—just that they make decisions and act with greater purpose and ease, which generally contributes to both greater confidence and deeper contentment.

At least that's what I'm betting on.

I experience this myself, most days. But it's even more evident to me when I *don't* live up to my principles. It's like someone has thrown sand into my gas tank. Nothing works quite as well, and I lose the sense of energy and peacefulness I get when I stay true to my core beliefs.

I also believe that what's true for an individual is true for companies and organizations of all sizes. Those with clear principles are often more effective and efficient because everyone knows what's expected and, therefore, what to do and what kinds of decisions to make. They adhere to their shared principles, making operating in this incredibly complex world much simpler, and that's not a bad thing.

Ten principles have guided VIA for over two decades—through the internet bubble burst of 2000, through periods of wonderful success, even through the Great Recession of 2007 to 2009. Not one word of our principles has changed. And they have served as counsel through all the issues we have confronted, helped us become resilient and inspired us to ever-greater heights.

I established our principles with VIA's two other founding partners, Rich Rico and David Puelle, one night in New York City near the end of our first year in business. We had talked for months about sitting down to craft them but kept putting it off. Because we tended to overthink everything, we imagined it would be a long and arduous assignment. And I think we needed that initial year of experience to really understand what we believed in.

We were staying in a cheap hotel in the middle of Times Square when we decided to stop procrastinating and start brainstorming. Just as we sat down to begin, the one smoker in the group stepped outside for a quick smoke before we dove in. The other partner and I opened up the laptop and decided to at least make a pretense of starting. I lobbed out "Be curious" as a starting thought. He nodded knowingly, and it seemed to unleash a flurry of very simple and clear statements about our beliefs. It was like magic. They just appeared before our eyes.

In 10 minutes we had nine principles written out. The door opened, our other partner returned, and we asked him to read them over. Now you have to understand that he was known as the team cynic, brilliant with a low tolerance for bullshit. He read the list, stopped for a moment, looked up at us with some disbelief and said, "That's it." Then he quickly added, "One more: Create respect. And then I think we can go eat."

Those principles are:

Be curious
Honor the process
Think like the audience
Create respect
Be on time
Be on budget
Figure it out
Find the magic
Do work that makes you proud
Believe

Those 15 minutes of effort ended up giving me the best return on investment of any time spent in my professional life.

I believe any organization can grow stronger and more successful through developing and adhering to its own set of principles. Our principles were designed to ensure that our agency would always be capable of solving complicated business challenges through greater collaboration and creativity. What follows is an exploration of those 10 principles' deeper meanings and lessons learned that might apply to any group or organization. Along the way I share stories we have lived through and clarify how our principles have helped VIA navigate the highs and lows of the mystifying and wonderful world of advertising.

1. Be Curious

*I think, at a child's birth, if a mother could ask a
fairy godmother to endow it with the most useful gift,
that gift would be curiosity.*
—*Eleanor Roosevelt*

Curiosity is the most beautiful of afflictions. Those blessed with a curious mind are always growing, never bored and usually pretty open-minded. Curious people tend to create harmony in the world, as opposed to intolerance, because they are smart enough to know there is always more to learn about anything. That's why "Be curious" is our first principle. It's a reminder to constantly stay interested in whatever new opportunities life presents. Those opportunities will require us to expand our views by asking questions and exploring the unknown.

I learned this early in life from my mother. As a stay-at-home mom raising seven children, she faced a lot of what many would consider drudgery. But she was always filled with enthusiasm and a fascination for all things in life. A voracious reader who loves talking to everyone she meets—and an expert questioner (some might even say interrogator)—she taught me this important secret: If we learn how to ask interesting questions we will never be bored. Her curiosity acts like a nuclear reactor in her heart, filling her with superhuman energy. The fountain of youth, as she demonstrates, is not somewhere in a swamp in Florida; it's in the wellspring of our own curiosity.

When in Doubt Always Ask Why

*Millions saw the apple fall, but Newton
was the one who asked why.*
—Bernard Baruch

If you take just one thing from this book, please take this: Always ask why. That simple act will ensure a lifetime of fascinating exploration. You'll never be stuck again. It's a question that takes you down endless paths, invariably leading to new and meaningful insights.

In 1996, VIA was riding the internet explosion and had landed a project to develop the website strategy for Sun Microsystems in Silicon Valley. It's hard to explain the feeling that permeated the business climate when the internet was brand new. There was unbridled enthusiasm for the changes it would bring to the world, but no one had a precedent or road map to follow. It was a moment in history like no other, so along with just about everyone in those days—everyone except perhaps Sun's then CTO Eric Schmidt, who later went on to run a little company called Google®—we were figuring out what to do on the web in real time. I interviewed Eric as part of our research and development process. To say I felt awkward telling him what his company's web strategy should look like is an understatement. I was pretty nervous about the meeting, but I went in armed with a simple weapon, the question "Why?"

I remember asking him why the internet was so important, why Sun was positioned to win and why he believed so much in technology. His answers surprised and enlightened me as he spoke of the independence of the various divisions of Sun and how the company's distributed structure allowed people to find the best solutions to problems. He also explained that Sun had core tenets for employees to follow with the aim of binding all the different divisions together. I found him to be a humble, lovely, brilliant guy. And the more the conversation turned to the reasons why, the more meaningful his answers became.

As we talked, the web strategy we should recommend became crystal clear. Defined in a detailed 100-page document, our solution could be boiled down to one simple idea: Sun should organize its external web presence around a concept much like our solar system (Sun, get it?). Give each division (planet) the freedom to operate its sections of the website individually to best serve its core markets while keeping all divisions linked (orbiting) in one system of shared standards (revolving around the Sun corporate tenets). Sun loved the idea, and the resulting new website became one of the most robust and copied corporate web structures of that era.

Asking why is the best tool in the curious person's bag of tricks. Sometimes it takes a little courage to ask this simple question because it might make people feel uncomfortable. But that's why it's so powerful. It can cut to the core of things, where the best answers usually hide.

FEARLESS CURIOSITY SETS US FREE

Life shrinks or expands in proportion to one's courage.
—Anaïs Nin

If we want to be true change agents, we must be curious. Curiosity builds diverse thinking, freeing people to discover and follow their most powerful callings. Unfortunately, many people live their lives in fear. "Better safe than sorry" is an all-too-common mantra. But developing a personal commitment to curiosity builds courage. And being open to new ideas can lead us to our own passions.

People in marketing roles on the client side work under enormous pressure. Their jobs are much harder and more complex than ours on the agency side. So it's understandable that fear can creep into their decision making, much like fear creeps into agencies when confronted with the prospect of losing a client if things don't go well. Many ideas don't even get discussed simply because people are too afraid for their job security to share something that might rock the status quo. But one way to mitigate the effects of fear in these situations is to hit it head on—call out the fear by putting it on the table. Have a direct conversation with the key decision makers about their fears. Once named, fears often seem less threatening or maybe easier to move beyond.

I first met Todd Pendleton as a new CMO at Samsung®, just after his stint at Nike, where he had successfully pulled off lots of amazing work. VIA was doing some strategy projects for the technology giant when I asked him what he was afraid of in his new position. He answered, "Having everyone here at Samsung get too comfortable with me. That means I am not pushing hard enough. I don't care if I get fired. I am afraid of NOT making an impact." When he walked away from Samsung it was after many successes and at the top of his game because he wanted the feeling of being uncomfortable again, facing huge learning curves and big brand issues. Instead of being happy with success and enjoying the fruits of his labor he was ready to jump back into the deep end. He wanted to challenge himself to do it again—only better. Being fearless about the unknown is a powerful idea to embrace.

Lucille Ball once said, "I'm not funny. What I am is brave." A little fearlessness goes a long way in developing curiosity. Putting what we have learned to the test can definitely cause jitters, but it's worth a try. If you're learning a new instrument, find the courage to play in front of someone. If you've learned some French, parle français every chance you get. If you make oddly curious crafts, show them to your friends. The worst that can happen is you will get judged, ridiculed and laughed at—by those who aren't curious. And that negative will be outweighed by something much more positive. The truly curious will benefit by learning from your courage to put yourself out into the world.

I was flying from New York to San Francisco once when I noticed that the man sitting next to me had a Bell Labs logo on his briefcase. A legendary and romantic icon in the world of research and scientific advancements, Bell Labs was a dream client of mine, so I wanted to find a way to spark a conversation. Scouring my memory, I vaguely recalled reading a story about one of Bell's scientists who had done some leading work in computer interface design, so I mentioned the story to the man. First he corrected me by accurately pronouncing his colleague's name, which I had read but never heard spoken. That made me feel a flicker of embarrassment. But then he said a wonderfully generous thing: "I don't mean to offend you. On the contrary, I think when a person mispronounces a name it is a sign of a curious self-learning." We talked for much of the flight, and that conversation led to VIA doing some fascinating marketing work for the voice recognition division of Bell. I have no idea why that article was rolling around in my head or where I had read it—that's not the point. What's important is that I put my fragment of knowledge out into the world to give it a chance to connect with an unforeseen opportunity.

Be a Hedonist of the Mind

I have never let my schooling interfere with my education.
—Mark Twain

I am a total dilettante and have dabbled in various creative pursuits most of my life. I've made lots of art, learned a couple of instruments, and written poetry and short stories—mostly with mediocre results, I don't mind admitting. But this wide range of trial and error has led to some of the most interesting ideas I've ever had. I can't overemphasize the value of exposing our minds to new forms of learning by living, and though I didn't receive one, I am a big supporter of a liberal arts education. Even more important than getting a formal education, however, is cultivating our own self-education throughout life. Cross-pollination of knowledge and experiences leads to bigger and more beautiful thinking.

By drawing on mixed knowledge gleaned from a cross section of experiences, we can solve new and complex problems; the greater the variety of vegetables to choose from, the more interesting the stew. I would bet on the curious generalist over the focused expert when it comes to tackling complex obstacles.

VIA Chief Creative Officer Greg Smith epitomizes this ability to blend new ideas from his wide and varied experience and knowledge. I remember watching one of his first pitches at VIA in which he quoted Emerson and Eminem in the same diatribe; referenced music by Debussy and Dr. Dre in the same breath; and then linked John Maynard Keynes' economics theories to Moore's Law to illustrate ways people would consume video content in the future. The wildly curious mind, exemplified by Greg, is capable of seeing new possibilities where more narrow minds see nothing.

To cultivate such a deep knowledge base, we can feed our brains hedonistically: Read fiction and nonfiction, poetry and *People* magazine, biographies and graphic novels. Watch all styles of movies and seek relationships with a wide range of people. One of my simple rules of life is to always be in the process of learning something new. It keeps me from falling into ruts, which are poisonous to curiosity.

Purpose Unlocks Curiosity

Older people sit down and ask, 'What is it?'
but the child asks, 'What can I do with it?'
—Steve Jobs

One of the greatest things a group's leader can do is keep reminding members of the purpose behind their collective efforts. Why? Because I think most people will work harder and smarter if they know their work matters. I read once in a Harvard case study that compensation is not the most meaningful factor in motivating corporate employees.

What is often more important to people is knowing they are involved in something meaningful, being kept well informed of the organization's efforts, and understanding how their work fits into the overall picture. From my experience, when people understand the roles they play in a bigger vision, it unleashes their natural drive to be curious because there is a reason to learn more and do more. Unlocking the potential in each and every person is actually the leader's most powerful tool, and it starts with the clarity of the shared purpose.

Insatiable curiosity often inspires visionary leaders. In 2000, former Maine Gov. Angus King (now a U.S. senator) shared his vision to provide every seventh- and eighth-grade student in Maine with a laptop computer to address the digital divide growing across the different socioeconomic groups in many communities and to potentially give Maine a long-term advantage in the marketplace with a more digitally literate population. This bold move was the first of its kind in the United States, and the governor had to do his homework to see if it was even viable. Because he knew I was spending a lot of time in Silicon Valley working with technology companies, he asked me to take him to visit the major tech players who might be curious enough to join his initiative.

Gov. King, his bodyguard, a staff member and I spent 10 days driving around the San Francisco area pitching his ambitious idea. Every company we spoke to had thoughts about how to best provide the technology solution using its own software and hardware, but each listed money as the biggest barrier to success. The last company we met with was Apple®. I didn't know anyone there, but their head of software development was a Mainer, and Maine is such a small place you can almost always find a friend who knows somebody whose cousin knows that person you want to meet, so we were able to get an audience with a few executives to talk about the plan. That meeting was different from all others that week. The subject of money never even came up. The people at Apple were so curious about our purpose that all they did was ask a ton of questions about the goals and vision for the project, called the Maine Learning Technology Initiative (MLTI). At the end of the meeting they said they needed to brief Steve (Jobs) about the project but definitely wanted to continue the conversation.

Apple committed significant time and resources to win the bid and became the technology provider for the MLTI, which went on to become an incredible model for the advancement of technology in education. The program's success was studied the world over by other forward-thinking communities.

Steve Jobs attended the ceremony to launch the program in Maine. Before the festivities began I got to spend some time with him, an especially meaningful experience because I had been a die-hard Apple user since 1984. That was the year I worked as an Apple rep on my college campus, trying to hawk the new Macs to poor college students—toughest sales job I ever had, which I told him. He laughed and said I should have just dropped out of the university and invested my tuition in Apple stock. "*Now* you tell me," I replied.

He was dressed in his iconic black turtleneck and blue jeans. But his reputation for being intense and volatile seemed hard to believe, as he remained extremely calm and present while we chatted about topics ranging from politics to design. I had studied the Apple case study in business school and knew quite a bit about the company,

particularly its clear purpose, which I had always equated with the secret to Apple's success. In speaking about the company's purpose in the book *Becoming Steve Jobs* by Brent Schlender and Rick Tetzeli, he said, "Our whole company is founded on the principle that there is something very different that happens with one person, one computer. ... What we're trying to do is remove the barrier of having to learn to use a computer." When I asked him why Apple had pursued the MLTI bid so aggressively, he looked at me and said simply, "We didn't have a choice. We had to win this bid. Everything we have ever done at Apple has led to this kind of opportunity.
I am dying to see how it all plays out." Steve Jobs seemed to embody the link between purpose and curiosity, illustrating that they go hand in hand and can lead us to astounding new places.

2. Honor the Process

Ah, the creative process is the same secret in science as it is in art. They are all the same absolutely.
—Josef Albers

I've spent over 20 years of my career as an advertising exec, but my dirty little secret is that I'd never stepped foot in an ad agency before the day I started VIA. I earned a bachelor's degree in mechanical engineering, and my first job was as a process control engineer. You might wonder how that background could have prepared me for a field as creative as advertising. And that's a fair question. Actually, it was the fundamental training in engineering that taught me how to solve problems. I wasn't the greatest engineer in the world, but engineering taught me some skills I now depend on heavily, logic and a methodical means for attacking any challenge. I knew nothing about running an ad agency when I started VIA, so I had to derive a method for doing it every step of the way. The realm of advertising can be intoxicatingly inspiring and loose, but it was methodical problem-solving that allowed me to survive in this business, and even thrive on occasion.

Working in advertising, I am surrounded by people who depend first and foremost on their instincts. I am a huge believer in instincts developed from past experiences but not at the expense of seeing the uniqueness of each situation. We can always benefit from stepping back and approaching any opportunity as though we've never confronted it before. When we depend too much on experience, we can miss opportunities for true innovation or simply overlook the most obvious answers.

One of the first clients VIA won was a large industrial manufacturer of printing presses headquartered in Germany. A breakthrough opportunity for us, the assignment was to create a campaign to launch the company's latest technology. Instead of honoring the process, we jumped to a creative solution rich with poetry and exquisite, artful imagery yet so far off the mark for this technically conservative company that it was laughable in hindsight. We did not *honor the process*. We didn't ask good questions. We didn't have respect for an industry we were strangers to. We didn't understand the constraints or conditions necessary for the campaign to be successful. Our hubris led to failure, but it's why "Honor the process" became one of our principles. We're never poorly served by looking at things thoroughly. Following the basic steps toward good problem-solving will help us create effective and fresh ideas and answers.

The Liberation of Constraints

The more constraints one imposes, the more one
frees one's self. And the arbitrariness of the constraint
serves only to obtain precision of execution.
—Igor Stravinsky

I often hear people say that process can limit creativity, but I don't buy it. When the structure of a sonnet was developed, did it limit the poet's creativity? I think creativity flourishes against the constraints it confronts. The mind and imagination have the ability to find answers in nearly endless variations when facing limitations.

Every new situation deserves fresh consideration of how to best confront it, and following a good process doesn't limit problem-solving or creativity; it frees it. The core approach almost everyone takes to problem-solving includes the following steps:

- Define the problem
- Research the situation
- Develop a hypothesis and ideas
- Test and analyze results
- Improve and execute the solution

These fundamental steps are found in almost every process that consulting companies often claim as "proprietary." In fact, they are all just veiled versions of the scientific method and not that proprietary after all. The hard part isn't creating a process; it's sticking to it.

Interestingly, good problem-solvers aren't necessarily the brightest people in the room but those who know how to design the right process for the situation at hand. For example, when confronting a challenge that must be addressed quickly, the key is knowing how to follow the basic problem-solving process in a shorter time period. Asking and answering a couple of questions upfront can help design a faster process: How can we design a process that allows for gathering *some data* versus *all* the data? Or one that works with fast ideation versus longer periods of exploration? In the end, following a quicker version of the process on a shorter timeline still beats taking a guess. In other situations, developing a longer and more thorough process will be appropriate.

A nonprofit focused on improving high school graduation rates for college-ready students approached us once for an advertising campaign focused on sophomores and juniors. Interested in helping address such an important topic, we designed a more comprehensive process to dissect the issue and gain a deeper understanding of the problem.

By researching the topic, analyzing the data and speaking to teachers, students, parents and administrators, we found that targeting sophomores and juniors would have little impact. If students weren't already on a college track leaving middle school, it was too late in most cases. We realized we needed to target middle school students and inspire or challenge them to get serious sooner so they could enter high school already enrolled in a college-track curriculum.

To reach the middle school audience, we created a TV campaign and game show called *Kick Start* that won an Emmy for its innovative content; devised fun online gaming platforms to match students to colleges that fit their personalities; got colleges to send letters of encouragement to those young and often neglected students; and gave away swag such as black concert-style *Kick Start* T-shirts, which students could only get by meeting with a guidance counselor for a college chat. We totally changed the game by remaking the game, which was possible only because we had designed the right process to uncover the true constraints of the situation. And that made all the difference in countless kids' lives.

Collaboration Stacks the Deck

Alone we can do so little; together we can do so much.
—Helen Keller

It's pretty obvious that today's companies face more complex problems and opportunities than ever before. Solving complex problems, I believe, requires exceptional collaboration. So the power to manage diverse skill sets in harmony becomes one key to success in our times. We can solve extraordinarily complex problems as long as everyone's voice is heard, differences are respected and a shared vision is maintained. We've just got to believe that we're better off depending on others than going it alone, and I always think we are.

The trick is harmonizing people's many differences. For example, in most industries today (as in advertising) the driving force of technology is increasing the rate and complexity of change. Managing people with a technical disposition alongside people with a creative disposition may seem difficult to some. But establishing shared principles helps people remain open and respect others' differences rather than view them as barriers. "Honor the process" is a principle that reminds us how much we all benefit from having clear steps for working through intricate challenges that demand exceptional collaboration.

Working with a large financial services company, we once launched a campaign that required us to develop new ad creative based on the morning's news and run it by end of day, a process that typically takes months, not hours. This Herculean task was further complicated by the strict compliance regulations that apply to the financial services sector. But getting the integrated client and agency team to agree to a few simple tenets made this nearly impossible task achievable. Those tenets were: commit to the daily regimen, designate a decision maker if you are unavailable, overcommunicate, and favor yes over no. We even made the lawyers comfortable with this breakneck-paced program because everyone worked collaboratively honoring the process.

A collaborative initiative is most powerful when everyone works in an open and timely manner. I know many people thrive under pressure and can't begin an assignment until the deadline looms large, but in collaborative businesses, that delay screws everybody else in the collective creative process as they sit around waiting for others to chime in or finish their parts of the job. Collaboration, like a big garden, must be tended well if it's to strengthen our work. Observe how collaboration works best for your culture, and also, as I will address later, know when too much of it can threaten your success.

Conflict Is Not a Four-Letter Word—Dick Is

A good leader can engage in a debate frankly and thoroughly, knowing that at the end he and the other side must be closer, and thus emerge stronger. You don't have that idea when you are arrogant, superficial, and uninformed.
—Nelson Mandela

In reality, conflict can arise when working through any process— difficult endeavors almost always become messy somewhere along the way. Encountering new issues and barriers is inevitable. The key is to make sure that people know conflict is OK and, even more importantly, that conflict should be celebrated as a critical part of the process as long as it's productive.

All too often conflicts crumble into fighting and personal attacks, which rarely create the best solutions. As my thoughtful friend Jim Fallon says, "The first one in business to get angry loses." I think people who use anger to bully or intimidate are showing their weaknesses. It is nearly always better to keep a level head if we want to guide people through conflict to a better outcome.

That only happens when people learn *how* to work through conflict constructively. Conflict doesn't have to include personal attacks. Conflict is about the collision of information, ideas and observations, which live independently from the personalities and characteristics of any individual.

It's important for people to respectfully critique ideas and constructively debate issues while talking about the work. Leaders, in particular, have to show true and authentic care for the people they're leading. If individuals know they are supported, respected and valued, conflict can be exhilarating, not damaging. Unchecked conflict in the absence of a caring environment can break down an organization's ability to grow and innovate. But with a level of care and purpose, there isn't anything a group of passionate people unafraid of conflict can't tackle.

Once during the "question and answer" section of a pitch with a big prospective client, VIA Chief Creative Officer Greg Smith and I simultaneously answered an interesting question posed by the client. The problem was we answered it differently—with strong points of view that didn't align. We then started an intense yet respectful argument over the merits of our conflicting points of view. You could feel everyone at the table sort of slide back to avoid getting caught in the fray. Normally, this kind of conflict is considered a major new-business faux pas; "thou shalt never break ranks in front of a client."

However, our interaction ended with Greg saying that my populist ideals were clouding my thinking, but maybe I had a point. Everyone laughed, and Denise Karkos, representing the prospective client, later told me that in that moment she decided to hire us because she knew we would push her business—respectfully and probably in a downright entertaining way most days. Over the years since then she has been a client on and off and always a friend even through many constructive conflicts.

These Things Just Don't Happen

Plan your work for today and every day, then work your plan.
—Margaret Thatcher

As a player and coach, Bill Russell led the Boston Celtics to two championships, a feat only he has accomplished. Brilliantly commenting on the intuitive touch needed to create a successful process, he once said, "The Celtic 'system' was designed to permit intelligent, winning players to endlessly use their own curiosity and creativity to accomplish results. That was why each of the players felt such an extraordinary commitment to the team. It was a living, everyday thing, a practice far more than a promise; it was their team." His leadership practices on and off the court inspired the best from everyone around him, and he always knew how much playing time he should get, and when to get out of the way and let his players shine. That level of self-awareness can help any leader succeed.

Because leaders and senior executives are ultimately responsible for how things are run, it is their job to develop a clear plan or process for everyone to follow. But how the process is executed and by whom becomes a balancing act. As is often said, a fish rots from the head.

If things aren't working well in your world, start by looking in the mirror and asking, "Am I the problem?"

There is no formula to tell us how involved we should be in the process we've designed. But it takes experience to know how to play our position well, and how much or how little playing time is right for us to ensure that our team wins. Often when senior people get too involved in the process, junior employees don't learn how to take initiative and therefore don't grow. Other times, when senior people don't lend enough of their talent and expertise to the process, the work suffers, things get overturned near the end after much effort by the team, and everyone is demoralized. Leaders need to set expectations for teams and clearly define success, then offer the right contribution to the process without stifling the team or impeding work.

One of the biggest leadership mistakes I've seen that reduces operational efficiency is failing to establish a clear decision-making process from the outset. Without a good decision-making process in place at the start of assignments, we often end up dealing with chaos by the time we realize we need one. And too much time gets wasted by decisions not being made, decisions being overturned or the wrong people making decisions. So before undertaking any big endeavor, while people are calm and rational, leaders should tell the whole team when decisions will be made and by whom. If you're on a team and that doesn't happen, raise a red flag right away and be a hero by saving everyone a lot of pain down the road. Although it's a simple first step, leaders sometimes hurry and skip it. Taking the time to complete that step will lead to more efficient and effective operations for clients and their partners.

One of the best tools in our agency toolbox is the client playbook, a one-page document listing the key strategic and process-related information necessary for everyone to stay on the same page. We've won many pitches because clients can tell that our entire team is in lockstep, and that comes from all working off the same playbook. As simple as it sounds, this powers the team through complicated processes.

Typically a playbook contains:

> **Purpose:** What the organization believes in
>
> **Vision:** Where the organization hopes to end up
>
> **Mission:** What the organization does day in and day out
>
> **Core message:** The heart of the organization's unique story
>
> **Audience:** Those we are targeting and communicating with
>
> **Goals/Objectives:** Quantifiable targets and completion dates
>
> **Strategic initiatives:** How and why we will win
>
> **Creative platform:** Inspiring transformational idea
>
> **Tactical actions:** What we are doing
>
> **Decision making:** Who makes the call

Like a sports team, every organization can benefit from having its own unique playbook. Make one. Follow it. This act is the essence of honoring the process, and if we do this, I am confident we will win more often than not.

3. Think Like the Audience

I do not ask the wounded person how he feels, I myself become the wounded person.
—Walt Whitman, "Song of Myself"

Most problems I see companies confront boil down to poor communication. It's amazing how hard it is sometimes for us to make ourselves understood. The natural human tendency is for us each to see and hear everything through our own filter; all our life experiences give us our frame of reference for analyzing the situations we find ourselves in. But that doesn't ensure understanding. It often leads to misunderstanding, the root of most problems.

What would the world be like if we all had a deeper understanding of the people in our communities, companies and families? I think it would be a much better place.

There is profound wisdom in the idea of trying to imagine walking a mile in another person's shoes. So why is it so hard to actually do it? Our principle "Think like the audience" is our way of consistently trying to see the world through the other person's eyes.

We each have a personal story that tends to inform how we think and act. When two people try to communicate, they sometimes make rash judgments and decisions about each other that don't lead to better understanding. I find that I communicate more successfully after spending some time contemplating the other person's situation. That requires slowing down and asking more questions, then actively listening to the responses and trying to be open to the other person's differences as opposed to being judgmental. If we study another person's history more carefully, it can help us find common ground, which usually leads to connection and, more valuable, insights that fuel truly transformative ideas. And that's the amazing gift that comes from thinking like the audience.

Love Listening

Well, some people without brains
do an awful lot of talking, don't they?
—*Scarecrow,* The Wizard of Oz

The art of listening turns out to be much more complex than I thought when I was younger. To be a great listener takes incredible focus and attention. Words, after all, can have various meanings.

Listening with our eyes and our entire being helps us pick up things words can't convey. It's been a lifelong effort for me to become a better listener, and as I've gotten older, I hope I have. I talk less and pay attention more, mainly because what I have to say seems less interesting than the new things others have to share. I think we all have the ability to improve our listening, and when we do, our understanding of the world will become richer.

I spent much of my youth on a basketball court. I wasn't the most gifted athlete, but my love of the game made it easy to spend hours and hours playing and trying to get better. As a senior in high school I was on a great team with a perfect regular-season record. I was not a starter for the team, but I was the consummate sixth player coming off the bench to fill in as needed.

At the end of the season, I won an award for "most improved." At first I felt embarrassed. At the apex of one's career, who hopes to be most improved? You hope to be the MVP. I nervously accepted the award and then stuck it in the back of my closet. But as the years went by, I realized it was a nice recognition, and a good reminder for me. I think it was the beginning of understanding that great listening has huge value. I had always tried to listen to the coach and practice what he told me to. Anyone willing to do that gets better. We simply have to be open to hearing what we're being told.

Go Live in the Wild

The question is not what you look at, but what you see.
—Henry David Thoreau

If our goal is to gain the deepest understanding of the people we interact with, we will discover endless layers of knowledge to absorb. We can begin to understand those layers by reading about people and their circumstances or listening to people talk about their situations, but nothing is more powerful than immersing ourselves in the environment where our audience lives every day. One of the most profound examples of immersion is the lifelong work of Dr. Jane Goodall. The depth of her study to understand the lives and behaviors of chimpanzees made the entire world see those incredible creatures differently. Because she went to such extraordinary lengths to exist alongside them, she didn't need words to understand how they lived and operated. She gained understanding by committing herself completely to their environment.

Immersion can make life more interesting on many levels. But it takes initiative, and maybe a little courage, to jump into new situations. Our agency has had the good fortune to work with the family-owned Perdue Farms. The chicken business, surprisingly, is one of the most complicated industries we've supported. To make sure everyone working with Perdue would understand and respect those complexities, Jim Perdue, the third-generation CEO of the company, wanted the whole VIA team to go through "Chicken 101," an immersion in everything that goes into bringing the perfect oven roaster to your family's Sunday dinner table. It was a little overwhelming to see each and every step in the process, from the chicks in the hatcheries to the hens running around the farmyard to the processing plants where the chickens are killed to the final test kitchens where the food is prepared.

Seeing the operation in its totality is humbling and gave us a new appreciation for how much work it takes to feed a nation. To do it right and do it well requires respect for the animals and the employees, and a slavish commitment to quality. It's all done on an enormous scale because there are so many people depending on this food source. So in the end, our job isn't just to make clever ads that try to sell chicken. We are part of a mission to help people deeply appreciate all that goes into making quality food for a family. The only way we can understand and communicate that is to know as much as we can about the business.

The immersion technique can benefit any part of our lives where we need to better understand someone different from us. My advice is to be slow (very slow) to judge others and fast (very fast) to dive headfirst into their situations and try to gather some real insight and empathy. No matter what we do for work, I believe that developing more empathy will make us better at our jobs. It's imperative if we want to make advertising that moves people. But even more imperative if we hope to bridge the gaps that keep us from making a better and more just world for all.

BEING THE SAME IS SO BORING

*It is time for parents to teach young people early on
that in diversity there is beauty and there is strength.*
—Maya Angelou

There's a very simple reason why diversity adds enormous value to any organization. We no longer live in an age when one point of view could address all the highly systemic challenges of the day. Every entity faces complex situations, and to operate effectively companies need diverse knowledge and skills to address a broad spectrum of issues they deal with on all fronts. Benjamin Franklin was such a prolific inventor partly because he lived in a world that had not yet embraced technology. That allowed for one person to capture decades of opportunity in a moment. That era has long passed. Technology has since exploded access to and integration of information, complicating everything so much that no one can take command of every dimension of today's multifaceted challenges. That means the more perspectives we consider, the more clearly we'll see our opportunities. Though it often seems forgotten these days, one of America's greatest strengths is its melting-pot heritage. Our unbelievable success over the last few centuries has come from the pragmatic understanding that through diversity, we create strength. It's better to have all our bases covered—it seems obvious, but we still shy away from it. Being with people like us almost always seems easier and more comfortable at least on a superficial level. But that doesn't necessarily make it better. A little dissonance can make music more interesting, art more compelling and life much richer.

Diversity comes in many different forms. Advertising, for instance, seems to attract boisterous and loud people. I've sat in many meetings where I sensed that the best idea or most thoughtful insight was trapped inside the brain of one of the more reserved, quiet people at the agency. Simply fighting to give more introverted people space and time to share is a form of championing diversity. For some reason, as obvious as the benefits of diversity might be, it's a constant battle to maintain it. Bigotry tends to plague our society, and even a little in seemingly mild forms diminishes our humanity. A lack of diversity in our thinking keeps it small—not to mention boring. Who wants the same old, same old when we can spice it up with something new?

Immediately after college I got a job at a global technology company operating in nearly every country worldwide. My first assignment took me to Germany, where I was put on a team with people from Pakistan, India, Ireland, China and Germany tasked with using our diverse experiences and skill sets to install state-of-the-art computer automation systems in old industrial mills. I was the minority of that group in terms of being the only greenhorn, so I had lots to learn on the job about tackling big technologically sophisticated projects. But my greatest education came from the conversations carried on by that diverse group at the beer hall in the evenings.

I listened to the Germans talk about their collective guilt over the Holocaust, the Muslim Pakistani reveal his current hatred of the Jews, the man from India blame the Pakistanis for his people's blights, and the Chinese woman talk about how the Western world was ignorant of her region's history. Even our happy-go-lucky Irishman late one night after a pint, or four, started reliving some of the sadness and discrimination he had suffered growing up in Belfast. As uncomfortable as many of those face-to-face conversations got, I promise that our two-month experience changed every person in the group for the better. We all gained understanding even if we didn't change our opinions completely. My time with that eclectic group altered my course in life for the better because it showed me how much I had to learn—and pointed me down a path that would be anything but boring.

At VIA, we encourage and embrace ideas that reflect the world's diversity, and we strive to create a diverse workplace. We are not diverse enough yet, but I expect all future leaders of the agency to fight to make the shop as diverse as possible. Without that, our work will become irrelevant at best, boring at worst. And boring advertising, like boring ideas, is a form of pollution.

SYMPATHY IS PASSIVE, EMPATHY IS ACTIVE, COMPASSION IS TRANSFORMATIVE

I want us to organize, to tell the personal stories that create empathy, which is the most revolutionary emotion.
—*Gloria Steinem*

Think for a second about the definition of sympathy versus empathy. It's a piece of cake to be sympathetic. Our brains can do it in an instant. It's easier because there's a lack of commitment to it; there's no real engagement needed to be sympathetic with a situation. But being empathetic—that takes real work. To feel someone's situation instead of simply intellectualizing it is an enormously different undertaking, maybe impossible. We can empathize with situations we've personally experienced more easily, but to empathize with someone whose situation we can't begin to understand is a much harder task. Yet it's essential to try if we are to think like the audience.

The hardest marketing challenge our agency has ever had to solve came from Larry Silverstein, the owner of the World Trade Center. On September 11, 2001, the disaster that took thousands of lives and destroyed the Twin Towers in New York City shocked the world and ushered in a new era of fear. Five years later, Silverstein Properties hired VIA to help market office spaces in 7 World Trade Center, the first tower to be rebuilt at ground zero.

An extremely successful developer, Larry Silverstein understood the real estate market better than anyone in the city. Yet with less than a year to the building's completion, no tenants were contracted to occupy the building. Our job was to help find organizations willing to move into that overwhelming and emotionally loaded location. I remember when we won the account thinking, "Is this a good thing or a bad thing?" because I wasn't sure we could solve the problem of getting people to move back to ground zero. But we kicked off the project, employing the principle "Think like the audience" as best we could.

By listening and immersing ourselves in the situation, we learned that people were simply afraid to work there. It took a little longer than usual to gain that key insight because at first no one would say it out loud. They talked about the long periods of construction, the uncertainty of the economy and the potential cost. Each of those problems I could sympathize with. But when I really imagined myself in their specific situation, I empathized with their unspoken fear. As is often the case, once a fear is named, it becomes less scary.

By empathizing with people's concerns, we were able to identify the kind of fearless leader this special location needed, the kind of leader who saw it as an imperative to move an organization to ground zero. This kind of leader understood that the act of relocating a business or organization to 7 World Trade Center signaled the forward-thinking nature of the group, the fearlessness of its cause and the pioneering spirit to capture opportunities where others saw peril. The nontraditional campaign we created and launched inspired leaders like that. Our efforts helped Silverstein Properties and its brokers achieve a 70 percent leasing level of the building in about nine months. The first tenant to sign on was the New York Academy of Sciences. When the organization's CEO spoke at the groundbreaking, he said, "Once again, science leads the way. We are leaders with vision. And this is our office."

Without empathy, we can't garner the insights needed to develop revolutionary ideas. But to effect real change we need compassion; it's empathy put into transformative action. When we are compelled to act with a deep sense of compassion, I truly believe we can improve any aspect of our world.

Caring Is an Amphetamine

*Unless someone like you cares a whole awful lot,
nothing is going to get better. It's not.*
—*Theodor Seuss Geisel*

It takes great effort to connect with an audience foreign to us. But the challenge of connecting with people lives at the heart of nearly every organization in the world. If we are doing things that don't ultimately help people, are they really worth doing?

My friend Mark Swann is one of the best entrepreneurs I know, and he chooses to operate a nonprofit. The year I started VIA, Mark was named the first executive director of a fledgling soup kitchen called Preble Street in Portland, Maine. Under his leadership, Preble Street has gone on to help thousands of the most needy members of our community: battered women, people with substance abuse problems, the homeless, people with mental illness, runaway teens—unfortunately, the list goes on and on. At Preble Street, Mark has developed many first-of-a-kind, nationally recognized programs to address some of society's most protracted and difficult plights. His secret? Massive caring. Mark's capacity to care about everyone he meets—especially the homeless, whose existence society often ignores—is astounding. He never turns away a soul or judges anyone, and he is quick to engage and embrace people who would make many of us uncomfortable. Mark's greatest strength is that he cares so deeply about people it energizes him to do the superhuman. Caring is his drug of choice.

So if we want to influence an audience, we need to care about that audience—and care a lot. We need to reach out, embrace, learn and understand, and when we do that across all dimensions of life, we gain the power to transform.

One of the greatest transformations we ever worked on was with a grocery chain in Florida called Kash n' Karry. Classy, right? In a world of upscale, more food-savvy customers, the tired brand needed a total makeover—a reinvention—which is one of the hardest things to pull off in any business. Luckily, the company's visionary EVP of Marketing, Steve Smith, cared deeply about the brand and knew it could be done. Partnering with him, we talked to everyone involved with the business at all levels: the people at the cash registers, in produce and meats, and out back in stocking, plus the entire management team. We went deep to learn what the customers cared about as well. This total team commitment translated to the most dramatic reimagining of a company we have ever done. It started with renaming the grocer Sweetbay, but that was just the beginning. We reinvented every tiny aspect of the brand. Every interaction had a new look, story and feel; right down to how we encouraged associates to take charge with four simple operating tenets: jump in, make the call, look around, and know your stuff. The rebirth was a dramatic success, winning a place on the Rebrand 100 as one of the top turnarounds in the world. That's what can happen if we truly care about what we do.

If someone working at VIA doesn't really care about our purpose or like the advertising business that much, and just keeps the job because it's a comfortable place to work, I try to do that person the favor of helping him or her find a new job with an organization that will be a better match. It will be a win for both the individual and the agency. We've got to find work we care about, or we are slowly dying and don't even know it.

Unlocking access to the things we find important releases a fantastic reservoir of energy. That power can help us do amazing things, things that enrich not only the people we serve but also our own understanding of ourselves—perhaps the most important audience we'll ever have.

4. Create Respect

*Setting an example is not the main
means of influencing others; it is the only means.*
—*Albert Einstein*

As I mentioned earlier, "Create respect" was the last principle we added to our list. But I could argue that it's actually the most important. I learned respect from my father, although he never demanded it from me, or anyone for that matter. People have respected him simply because of how he lives and who he is: humble, hardworking, caring and committed. What's not to respect about that? He worked for the Maine Department of Transportation for 61 years (yes, six one), starting as a field surveyor and going on to be the chief engineer leading 600 engineers at one time, then quietly working as a special expert resource to the department until he was well into his 80s. The whole time, he created respect by doing his job well. He shuns attention, so when the state of Maine decided to name a major stretch of highway after him, he was mortified. He had created that much respect over the years—to deserve such an honor—not by seeking it but by living according to his principles.

Respect plays a role in many dimensions of business and in any healthy relationship. To be respected in advertising we have to make work that others wish they had made or have a reputation for being a strong competitor. The latter seems like one of the most superficial aspects of respect, but we humans can't seem to shed our egos long enough to resist a bit of swagger. Back in the mid-1990s we were competing for some business in Silicon Valley and had made it to the finals. In those days we hadn't yet opened an office in San Francisco, so my partner and I decided to save a little money by sleeping on the beach at Half Moon Bay the night before the pitch. In the morning we bummed a shower off a guy with a camper and headed to the client's headquarters. To say we looked a little rough around the edges would be kind.

As is often the case, we had to wait in the lobby for our turn to present because the client was running very late. Members of a competing agency—a red-hot West Coast group that was the first real digital-only shop in the country—arrived, signed in and read that the agency pitching before them was from Maine. Maine? Assuming we were already inside presenting (never imagining people as unkempt as we were could be in the glamorous advertising world), their team began making jokes about the "clam diggers" they were pitching against and how they were going to kick our ass. When the client came out to the lobby to escort us into the presentation, they realized that we were the Maine agency. On my way by, I wished them good luck and handed them my card, an expired clam-digging license, before entering the conference room. We won the assignment and a little West Coast respect as well.

However, the respect gained from winning doesn't matter nearly as much as the respect earned from how we treat people and how we behave when no one is around. This principle serves as a key reminder that everyone deserves respect. Our clients deserve respect just as we deserve respect. The people we communicate with and their communities deserve respect. Even the work we struggle to create deserves respect. It's our expectation, as this principle clearly suggests, that as a company we will always behave with complete integrity. It's actually for a very simple reason—if we behave with integrity, we don't have to play games and get entangled in lies or nefarious situations that never lead to anything good.

A Golden Rule

Do unto others as they wish, but with imagination.
—Marcel Duchamp

As I started writing this book and thinking about the broader meaning of VIA's principles, I realized that our "Create respect" principle is perhaps just our version of the golden rule: Do unto others as you would have them do unto you. Pretty straightforward. Treat others the way you would want to be treated.

Many people seem driven to try to take advantage of others, mostly out of fear that others may take advantage of them first. Political backstabbing is a cancer in many organizations and certainly in some of our systems of governance. Being overly political and driven to take unfair advantage of others isn't the same as being appropriately competitive in a capitalist society. Competition is a fact of nature. Yet it can still be handled with a level of fairness and compassion that ensures a greater good. Some may view this as paradoxical, but I don't. I believe one should compete but never take unfair advantage of a situation. If you ever played sports, the things your coach taught you generally apply to business and life. Just play by the rules. Don't talk back to a ref. Help a fallen competitor get up. Shake your opponent's hand after a game. Be humble in victory. Accountable in defeat. Do unto others ...

After spending the first phase of my career in engineering roles, I wanted to get into sales. My first opportunity was in a support role providing financial analysis of the returns that could be gained from the installation of multimillion-dollar computer systems to run large manufacturing facilities. Sales of such large computer systems took months, often years, to close. And they were hugely competitive. Sales reps were often asked to camp out at a client's global headquarters while the company brought in competitor after competitor, trying to grind out the best deal possible. And because so much money was involved, I saw some pretty incredible stuff happen. Once, I was followed for an entire week by a private detective who had been hired by a foreign competitor to track my movements. What a boring gig, I thought, so in keeping with the "do unto others" mantra, I got in the habit of sending him a beer every time he showed up at the restaurant where I was dining. Like I said, compete, but always be a good sport about it.

The first computer sales pitch I worked on was led by an incredible young executive named Roger Bailey. He was the typical sales type, a big, good-looking jock with a whip-smart mind. And competitive. Very competitive. While traveling we played one-on-one basketball games that were outright death matches. He had orchestrated the team of people presenting our capabilities to a large corporation, and I got to play my small part talking about the potential return on investment the client could expect from our computer systems. When the meeting ended we all swept up our materials to clear the conference room for the next competitor. As we drove back to the hotel, recapping the meeting in the car, my boss asked me a question about our proposal. When I reached into my briefcase I saw an unfamiliar binder. I had accidentally grabbed a competitor's proposal from the conference room during our quick cleanup.

At first I felt exhilarated; that would give us a huge advantage in the pitch, and I excitedly told my boss what I had. He groaned, then calmly asked me how I had gotten it. I told him that someone had left it behind and I had mistakenly picked it up. He asked if I had looked inside it and I said no. Then he turned the car around to return the document. We took it in, told the prospective client what had happened and left. The next day the client told us we were out of the bidding process.

Why would I share this story? It has a really bad ending. But that's the point. The prospective client didn't trust that we were telling the truth. That client never invited us to another pitch, and it was a big loss for our company. But I tell this story because my boss was right. He did the right thing. Our integrity is defined by the things we do when no one sees us—when we do what is right regardless of the outcome. We do what we hope others would do for us. If everyone lived this way, the world would be a better place. It was a hard way to learn that lesson because I felt I had let my boss and team down. But it was an invaluable lesson to learn early in my career. And both my boss and I went on to have pretty great lives. In the long run, if we create enough respect, it always pays back priceless returns.

No Gossip Is the Best Kind of Gossip

*It is one of my sources of happiness never to
desire a knowledge of other people's business.*
—Dolley Madison

Sometimes it's the little things that erode respect. Alice Roosevelt Longworth was credited with saying, "If you haven't got anything nice to say about anybody, come sit next to me." And I get it. Gossip can be a recreational drug. There's something titillating about it, but it's one of the little things that can chip away at creating respect.
So it's important to do everything in our power to minimize the negative or useless comments many of us vent in moments of frustration. Though it's easier to be negative, blame others or see the problems they created, it's much more valuable to embrace the positive, focus on the opportunities ahead, and encourage and support people around us, especially those who might not be exactly like us. I try to do this to the best of my ability and have found that I literally feel better, even during very stressful times, when I focus on seeing the good in people and thinking about how to help them make things better instead of bitching about their shortcomings to others.

We've experienced painful moments at the agency when people did not live up to the expectation of "no gossip"—like the time an account person wrote a comment disparaging a client in an email intended for a VIA employee but accidentally hit "reply all." The client was very hurt by the comment but wise and strong enough to move beyond it with grace. However, it was hugely embarrassing to everything VIA stands for and deeply unfortunate that such a wonderful person was hurt like that. The lesson isn't to be careful with our email habits (though that is a good lesson too); the lesson is to avoid saying negative things about people to start with. I have little patience for people who constantly complain about clients. We should get another job if we don't respect the people who make our jobs possible.

To get the best results when groups collaborate in fast-paced environments, we should try to employ that age-old sentiment of giving people the benefit of the doubt. Try not to assume the worst. Instead, assume that everyone is trying hard, and we should be honest and forthright with our feelings about frustrating situations, not passive or aggressive. Also, we should make it clear that we want everyone to work together toward the best possible outcome for all. It can be hard to share constructive and kind comments in a world often dominated by the jaded or cynical. We run the risk of ridicule for being naïve, or even ignorant. But in the end, neither is true. Showing our ability to see everything for what it really is—connected —will empower us to find new ways forward where others will see only emptiness.

There Are Many Views From the Ship We Sail

The God who existed before any religion counts on you to make the oneness of the human family known and celebrated.
—Desmond Tutu

Tolerance is a word some people react negatively to because they think it implies putting up with something unpleasant—or that it is imbued with apathy, an attribute often distasteful to people who want to create change in the world. But my understanding of this word changed dramatically when I interviewed former Archbishop Desmond Tutu, a leader of the effort to end the apartheid system of segregation in South Africa, for my research project on leadership. I was conducting a series of interviews with prominent leaders, and he invited me to visit him at Emory College, where he was recovering from a battle with cancer.

I was surprised to find Archbishop Tutu to be physically smaller than I had expected (plus he was wearing a Hard Rock Café sweatshirt, which was not quite the garb I had pictured for such a reverent leader either), but he was big in spirit and immensely welcoming, warm and human. We started by sitting together and praying, something I hadn't done in a while. But I remained open to his way, and in the next hour or so he shared his beliefs on why tolerance and reconciliation are the only ways for humankind to move forward. His capacity to understand, forgive and embrace a more enlightened world order was humbling, to say the least.

During our conversation I learned that for him, tolerance is not blind acceptance of what is but rather a key to moving forward in a complicated world so that progress can be made even as things remain unbalanced—or unjust. In addition, only through reconciliation and forgiveness can mutual respect have a glimmer of hope of emerging from the shadows of past atrocities. It takes the bigger person to make that first step toward reconciling and moving beyond the horrors of yesterday. Though small in stature, Archbishop Tutu was the bigger person. He led his nation, taking the first step to allow people to progress toward forgiveness and a brighter future. If we want to be strong leaders, we must maintain the humility to always take the high road and accept the hard things that ultimately move us and our followers forward. That is the lesson I learned from the former archbishop.

"The capacity for or the practice of recognizing and respecting the beliefs or practices of others" is the definition of tolerance. Tolerance is necessary for creating respect. There are rarely simple rights and wrongs in our world. We have to assess and accept compromises in almost all decisions we make in any given day, but with an eye toward a better future.

In my early 20s I was perhaps as idealistic as a person that age can be. I was 30 when I started VIA, and my idealism was still extremely strong (the fact is, it still is today). But in the very first year of business I learned a lesson about idealism and tolerance that has stuck with the agency and me ever since. An employee had gotten a lead from a technology company that needed some marketing help. Great, right? Well, the company made software and equipment used to manufacture cigarettes, a product I personally hated. So I said we were not going to pursue the opportunity. End of discussion.

The next morning the woman working that lead came into my office and explained that members of her family were longtime tobacco farmers raised in tobacco country and that a team of people at VIA wanted to work on the business (one partner and even some nonsmokers). She felt strongly that it was wrong for me to project my values at the risk of the overall financial health of the agency and potentially people's job security.

I could have stood firm and been done with it. That would have been the easy way out. And there are times when we are absolutely justified in living by our personal ideals. But tolerance is a balancing act, so we raised the topic at an agencywide forum and had a passionate and invigorating dialogue about what was right, fair and beneficial to the agency and all employees.

We concluded with a set of guidelines for making controversial decisions like that moving forward:

- If a group of people at the agency want to take on a certain client, we will.
- No one will be forced to work on an account against a moral objection, but we can't guarantee employment if other work is unavailable.
- We won't do anything illegal (obviously, but it was discussed).
- We won't work with disreputable people or companies (tougher to define, but like pornography, we know it when we see it, and this gave me a chance to remind people that it was still my company and I had certain limits regarding what I could accept).
- We won't do political work because we are too diverse a company to represent one set of views.

This is not a perfect group of rules, and many gray topics still arise. But it has been a framework for talking about the company's plans for growth, and it's invoked rigorous and healthy dialogue over the years.

In the end, we did take on the assignment for the client that made technology for the tobacco industry, but I didn't work on the account. I still hate smoking. The team did some solid marketing for that client though, and the work kept some good people employed and made the person who had brought in the business very happy. But most importantly, it taught me to be a little more tolerant. I had to accept something about my company that wasn't 100 percent in line with my ideology. That tolerance, I think, has made me a better leader in the long run.

It's easier to live life in a little bubble including only people just like us. The problem is that's not the real world. Most businesses and communities have a broad spectrum of people and opinions. If we are going to change the world, we need to understand all aspects of it. Tolerance doesn't mean blind acceptance of things you don't believe in. It means recognizing and respecting the beliefs or practices of others. This is critical for working in a complicated world. Stick to our beliefs, yes; just don't write off the beliefs of others, or we may end up with limited change instead of transformative change.

Fighting for Respect

Our lives begin to end the day we
become silent about things that matter.
—Martin Luther King Jr.

Gray is the most pervasive color in the world. There's no such thing as black and white. As a situation gets grayer, we seem to get more adept at rationalizing why we love gray. But there are times when we have to make a stand for what we believe is right. I think the canary in the coalmine in such situations is when we get the first whiff of the stench of disrespect. Being open and tolerant is important, but sometimes we need to make decisions to protect our people, our organizations and ourselves from situations where respect has evaporated. Though it might feel easier to ignore a bad situation and let it creep along, fearing confrontation, once disrespect gets a foothold, it spreads like a plague. It will eat away at your organization before you realize what's happening.

Years ago, we won one of our first big, sexy accounts, a skiing company that operated mountains across the country. We were thrilled at the chance to help a great sport, and being able to ski after a client meeting didn't hurt either. The work went well for a while, and the client paid its bills on time—a plus because it was a big account for us. But their style and ours made for a very challenging relationship, which turned bitter and anything but respectful. My team felt humiliated and demoralized by the whole experience, and I am sure our client wasn't feeling so great either.

I knew what I had to do: resign a client for the first time. I think I could've rationalized sticking it out because it was a big account for us and we needed the money. It was a hard decision to make, but it was the right one. I saw what was happening to the people at VIA and how the disrespect they were experiencing was infecting the agency and spreading across all the accounts. I was probably a little too slow in taking this action, but I was amazed at how fast the positive impact on morale outweighed the financial burden it caused. In the end I learned that nothing's more valuable than fighting for the respect everyone deserves.

5. Be on Time

Eighty percent of success is showing up.
—*Woody Allen*

The next two principles, "Be on time" and "Be on budget," may seem perfunctory in their directness or a little limited in their guidance. But taken together, they remind us that the simple things are important. If we are not on time it sends a message of disrespect or indifference to those who end up having to wait for us. I've seen what feels like lifetimes wasted because meetings didn't start on time. Those squandered moments obviously can't ever be regained, and there's a subtle tragedy to that—countless precious hours wasted sitting in conference rooms because certain people didn't respect other people's time. Anyone can develop the habit of being on time. Even VIA's longtime Chief Creative Officer Greg Smith, self-described as often flaky, is always on time, because his father taught him "if you are not on time you will spend your life digging out of a hole." Being on time is a great gift we can give everyone in our lives—the gift of more time.

But the idea of time is obviously enormous, profound and deeply mysterious. Our science is still uncertain about what time really is. The one thing I know for sure about time, however, is that there never seems to be enough of it. Because of its scarcity, I place even greater importance on fulfilling my commitments and obligations so I can be efficient with the most precious of resources. Here are some ideas on how to make the most of our time.

Harnessing the Unstoppable

*The question isn't who's going to
let me; it's who is going to stop me.*
—Ayn Rand

For years, VIA's tagline was, "The difficult we do immediately. The impossible will be ready Thursday." To aspire to this cheeky statement, we had to become masters of time. How do we make the most of the time we have? Dissecting the practical elements of time helps us understand how to make the best use of it, but it takes practice to fully leverage that understanding. Basically, we have some control over three dimensions of time: when to begin something (initiative), how fast to do something (speed), and how to change or stop what we are doing (agility).

Initiative
Initiative is the dimension of time where new possibilities are born. That first step toward a new vision is perhaps the most magical and the most difficult to take. But it doesn't have to be. There are many reasons why people don't begin things they dream about. Fear of failure. Fear of not having all the answers. Fear of being ridiculed. The list of fears is long.

So how do we find the courage to overcome our fears of trying something? Learn to stop caring so much. Again, paradoxical, I know. To do something we really care about, we have to learn to care less. Yes. Stop looking toward the future all the time and just tackle the day ahead of us. I recently spoke at a conference with other entrepreneurs, and I was amazed that we all shared the same theme in our talks. None of us had any prior experience doing the work that was at the center of our new ventures. For example, one person had never designed textiles, another had never run a circus school, and I had never stepped foot in an ad agency before starting VIA. We all simply chose a point in time and began. Day by day we made mistakes. Day by day we got a little better. We achieved what we had envisioned by not fearing the future too much and just getting through each day as it came. So if you feel stuck, simply begin now.

Speed
One way to find more time is to move faster. The biggest change in our industry over the last 20 years is that everything has sped up. Everyone expects things faster and faster, so we need to be aware of our pace while working. Cultivating speed can give us a competitive advantage. Learning to strip unnecessary steps from a process, or simply doing everything faster, is a core requirement. But we must watch out for the times when rushing starts degrading the quality of our work. It's like running down a steep hill and feeling like you can't stop without turning into a train wreck. Yikes. But practice makes things fastest.

Agility
Pivoting in our work can prevent wasting valuable time. Understanding when to change our approach if it's not working, or when to eliminate unnecessary steps in our work or recognize better ways forward, can save huge chunks of time. Also, knowing

when to stop what we're doing is a form of agility. As singer and songwriter Lou Reed eloquently once said, "Stick a fork in their ass and turn them over. They're done." A lot of time is misspent overworking things that are done. Know when to stop.

A small but valuable example of solving a client's problem through mastery of those three dimensions of time began in a meeting with Norman Abdallah and Brandon Coleman, the very smart CEO and CMO of national restaurant chain Romano's Macaroni Grill®, about the best pricing strategy for an upcoming promotion. They asked VIA to recommend an optimal price point for the new offer. A typical pricing research study can take months, but they gave us only a week to figure it out. Initiative: We said we could do it. Agility: We pivoted by fielding a new technology to gather the data needed. Speed: We offered a quantifiably rationalized answer in four days—$14.75, in case you were curious.

Planning, Priorities and Patience

But seriously, I think overall in the scheme of things winning an Emmy is not important. Let's get our priorities straight. I think we all know what's really important in life—winning an Oscar.
—Ellen DeGeneres

Being on time first requires acknowledging that commitments must be met, and that requires planning. It seems to me that too often work gets done disproportionately closer to any existing deadline. So the reality is that people waste time procrastinating before a deadline—I have surely been the culprit in this in the past. At the same time, another (probably rarer) type of worker rushes to get the task done as soon as it's assigned. That too can waste time, because the pressure to complete the task feels more important than taking the time to do it well. To balance such extremes, I've always believed in adding a little patience to my planning. As we develop our approach to any new initiative, we should carefully ponder the time allocated. Too little or too much time for each step in the process can be damaging. I've found that good time management starts with understanding exactly what needs to be done and reviewing precedents, for example, by talking with people who've done the task before or studying previous experiences. Once we calculate the time needed to do the work, we should cut it by a third. I think it's always better to have *more* pressure in the system, not less. This bears repeating: Constraints, especially time constraints, can lead to resourcefulness and reinvention.

But almost every new day begins with too many items on the to-do list—and not enough time. To help set priorities, I developed a checklist for the busiest days. By following my checklist, I can spend my time on the most critical things first. I assess my tasks by categorizing them into five buckets:

- Crises
- Bottlenecks
- Deadlines
- Passions
- Everything Else

I deal with crises first. Whether it's a sick kid, an employee dealing with tragedy, or a client experiencing a dramatic business disruption, these time-sensitive issues obviously need to be addressed immediately. I always hope crises are the exception, not the rule. Keep in mind though that it's important to be able to assess a true crisis. Many people thrive on making *everything* a crisis, and it becomes an excuse for not being focused on more meaningful work that often gets ignored.

Next I look at tasks where I'm the bottleneck, keeping others from doing their jobs because they are waiting for me. I rank those fairly high on my priority list because it's fundamentally disrespectful to impede the progress of others on the job. The bottleneck tasks are often quite simple: a quick answer to a question, an approval on a budget or a brief assessment of someone else's work. But not doing them can hamper our organization's ability to operate quickly and efficiently.

The third category on my priorities list is pending deadlines. I tend to review my deadlines daily, which prevents having to cram at the last minute. I prefer to use the entire period allotted for an initiative, and regularly reviewing deadlines helps me spread my time out evenly. Still, there are times when I'm up against the wall, so my focus *has* to be on the next task required to meet a deadline and honor the "Be on time" principle.

The final and most important guideline I use in setting priorities is focused on the things I'm most passionate about. At some points during my life I have wasted time on things that didn't really matter to me (the "everything else" bucket). Perhaps because they were easy. Or maybe I wasn't being thoughtful, or my thoughts came from a place of confusion. Now I try to prioritize my time for the things most important in my life and favor those over more trivial tasks. On the job, I am most passionate about the health of the culture and the brilliance of the work. So I make sure those areas get my first attention and best efforts. Then after I attend to my passions I spend some time on the "everything else" bucket.

Every Idea Has Its Time

*Sometimes I arrive just when God's
ready to have someone click the shutter.*
—Ansel Adams

I've often felt there are no new ideas, simply the right time for certain ideas. Being on time can also mean being aware of the period we live in, staying current, and moving or growing with the culture of our day. Young people have an impressive ability to synthesize the edges of generational transition. Even before their own coming of age, many are able to observe the patterns, behaviors and ideas of the previous generation, then launch into their own time, reinventing the way their world works. It's critical to understand a time's influence on everything we do. I'd be willing to bet that every generation for the last 200 years thought they lived through the most tumultuous change in the history of humankind. Maybe that's true, or maybe it's simply that time has a way of churning life up and requires us all to stay current in order to grow.

A copywriter here once wrote that "VIA was born in 1993 and reborn every year since." To stay relevant we have to constantly develop and change, keeping abreast of the times. Nearly every project or assignment we've done has made us challenge old approaches and conventions to find new ways of operating. Failing to do that is the first sign of obsolescence.

Samsung, the world's largest consumer electronics manufacturer, once called us in to help launch a tablet aimed at competing with the extremely buzzworthy new iPad® from Apple. Samsung's primary agency of record had failed to devise a compelling campaign, and it was just five weeks until product launch. Apple had spent tens of millions of dollars advertising the iPad, yet Samsung was budgeting a small fraction of that amount for its competing campaign. Being late for the product launch wasn't an option. So we knew two things: We had only five weeks to deliver, and a traditional ad approach that would take months to deploy was wrong for the times. We took one key feature of Samsung's tablet—that it was half the size of the iPad—and translated that difference into a clear benefit. It provided freedom (through great portability) for the user, a timely theme for our country as we headed into a national election, when citizens would be able to exercise their freedom in the voting booth. Using only digital media, we literally invented two new advertising formats (we called them the "slurp" and the "walk off") that delivered innovative home-page takeovers of sites like NYTimes.com and CNN.com to create a disruptive campaign that referenced our culture and helped reinvent product launches in this new world's environment. It was the right approach for the times and helped establish the new Samsung tablet firmly in the crowded category.

Cultivating a sense of timing requires cultivating awareness. The best trend-spotters I have known possess incredibly intuitive awareness. They feel what is happening in the world around them, not just regurgitate what they have read or been told. We can all cultivate this awareness, but I think it takes slowing down instead of racing through the day to be open to the people and things around us. By quieting our minds occasionally, we can actually expand our views and understanding. There is great wisdom in a saying I heard years ago: "Sometimes we need to go slow to go fast." Slowing down gives us a chance to address the bigger picture, more completely attend to details that might trip us up in the future, or feel the underlying currents moving our culture forward. By going slowly sometimes, we afford ourselves the opportunity to discover the best idea for the times.

If we do slow down occasionally, when we speed up, we just might be able to fly, which is often the only way to be on time in today's fast-paced world.

Take the Long View

If you do nothing, you get nothing.
—Aung San Suu Kyi

I've shared some thoughts about how to make the most of the time we have, but how do we make sure we get as much time as we can? By being aware of our potential longevity. But it's hard to make things last, since human nature often draws us to do the things we are more certain will directly benefit us today than the things that might help future generations. It's a balancing act to know when to do things for the "now" versus the "later." However, if we don't care for the future we become a disgrace to our past. We owe much to the people whose sacrifices and advancements have made our world freer, more knowledgeable and more inspiring. But clearly there is endless work left to do, and it is our responsibility to be mindful of the future in our actions today.

Some companies focus too heavily on short-term profits because, in my opinion, they are driven by greed or a lack of imagination— both unhealthy. It's much smarter for businesses to prioritize long-term profits in concert with learning to operate sustainably and with less environmental impact; understanding how to create new opportunities to engage and employ more people as technology takes over more human roles; and creating more peace and security so freedom can ignite greater innovation and awakening. All these things must become part of companies' long-term business planning if we are to have any hope of creating the world we, and our children, deserve.

I have always thought the most practical long-term action an individual in a company takes is hiring a new employee. It's like adding a link in a chain to the future. If we hire good ones, our tomorrow will be strong. If we then forge them with great training and experiences, we'll endure well into the future. I have hired hundreds of people over the years; most have been incredible, but I will say my biggest mistakes in business have been connected to hiring the wrong people. Ever the optimist, I tend to see the positive in people during an interview and ignore their shortcomings; or I have been in such a hurry to fill a position that I made a rash decision. Following are a few suggestions to help hire the best people you possibly can so you can keep your company rolling into the future:

Hire slowly and fire quickly
Too often I've hired people without thoroughly vetting them, just hoping for the best. Then when someone started failing, I dragged out the termination, not wanting to hurt the person or disrupt his or her life. I wanted to be compassionate, but avoiding dealing with a bad fit doesn't do the company or the employee any favors in the long run. The best advice I can give here is to take the time to hire slowly but fire quickly when you know you need to make the move, something I've heard countless times. The trick though, as with all good advice, is actually putting it into practice.

Bring on people better than you
This might be one of the hardest things to pull off in business. Managers sometimes feel nervous about hiring candidates with more potential or skills for fear of being shown up. Equally true, great candidates rarely want to work for those who seem less capable than they are. But if we can put our egos aside and persuade brilliant candidates to join our cause, we usually end up with plenty of success to go around.

Don't hire people who are rude to servers
I once took a candidate for an executive position out to lunch as a final step in the interview process. Our conversation was fine, but I was uncomfortable with the way the candidate treated our lovely server like an indentured servant, barking orders arrogantly and dismissively. I made the hire hesitantly, as his talent was evident, only to discover within a few months that he was treating nearly the whole VIA staff the way he had treated that poor server. Talent is not an excuse for being a jerk. Hire talented, nice people (don't worry, there are plenty around), and it will definitely pay off in the long run.

Choose a mixed bag of nuts
One of the nicest things a client ever told me was that VIA seemed like the Island of Misfit Toys because we were such an array of eclectic characters. I'm not sure it was meant as a compliment, but I took it as one, as it is certainly what we have tried to build over the years. The first line I read on any resume I receive is the "Other Interests" section, not where the candidate went to school or worked last. I want to know where people's curiosity has taken them. If I read that someone collects pre-revolution Ukrainian glassware, makes custom guitar picks from oyster shells or performs stand-up comedy in prisons, I want to schedule an interview. If someone attended an Ivy League school and had some impressive jobs, but that's all? Next! Creating our own crazy little melting pot makes us as resourceful and interesting as our great nation and as entertaining as the circus, which I believe strengthens employee retention in a very real and amusing fashion.

Test by fire, train by example

When possible, test potential hires with tasks that prove they can deliver. We once gave a finalist for a senior client director position the simple task of presenting his past work to a small group. The person totally flamed out, and we held back the offer, saving us all a lot of heartache. In today's world, we need to effectively perform the tasks we claim we can. It seems obvious, but I have seen many people overstate their skills and talents. It's just too competitive for companies to carry people who can't deliver. But at the same time, you have to show people what is expected of them after they are hired. I remember once being in my kitchen trying to feed my 2-year-old as she sat distractedly in her high chair. It was a battle of wills to see who would crack first. Suddenly she started banging her open hand on her tray and screaming, "Shit, shit, shit!" When she saw the shock on my face she laughed hysterically. Well, that's when I learned the important lesson that your kids model what you do, not what you tell them to do—just like employees. To make our companies strong we need to invest time in having employees shadow people in relevant situations. We need to always model the behaviors we expect in daily activities and demonstrate our principles in the way we make important decisions. And it means making sure people have mentors who take the time to show them the ropes.

The founder of an organization should start thinking about succession planning on day one of a new venture because passing the reins to the next leader can be one of the hardest, most time-consuming tasks for an entrepreneur to achieve. When it came time for me to choose my successor as CEO, I knew that finding the right person would ensure VIA's success for decades to come. I was never more careful with a hire, employing all the points listed here. When I first met Leeann Leahy over lunch, not only was she kind to the server, but she made him laugh with her quick wit. She clearly had lots of talents and experience that I didn't, having been a consistent superstar at many top agencies. Talk about hiring slowly, I actually made her the agency president for three years to test her skills under fire. (Her first day on the job she took on the biggest client in the agency's history, which we had just landed, a huge test by fire.) And in the days and years following, she demonstrated her trustworthiness, grit and creativity. She even proved her eccentric nature, once taking the entire agency to a dance club—over lunch. Because I had taken the time to make sure she was the right person for the job, when it came time to announce her new role as CEO, we were all positive she would help VIA thrive well into the future.

Longevity is often underrated but is perhaps one of the most important goals of any organization. To be on time, day in and day out, is the secret to longevity. It helps us always move forward and turns time into our most powerful and lasting asset.

6. Be on Budget

A wise person should have money in his head, but not in his heart.
—Jonathan Swift

Money is a funny thing. It's just an idea, a simple commitment to recognize the value in the things we own, exchange and sell. But in the end, it's really nothing. Yet many people in the world spend most of their lives obsessed with money. I like money. I don't love money. So like everything, the key is paying the right amount of attention to the role money should play in life and business. "Be on budget" is a reminder to meet our fiduciary commitments to our clients as well as maintain balance and fairness in our dealings with money.

Always Invest, Rarely Spend

'People have forgotten this truth,' the fox said. 'But you mustn't forget it. You become responsible forever for what you've tamed. You're responsible for your rose.'
—Antoine de Saint-Exupéry, The Little Prince

When a client hires VIA, it's not just to make creative stuff. It's to help grow their business. We should think of VIA as a money management firm, not an ad agency. For every dollar we are given, we should create a positive return for our client's investment. The overriding question should be, "What is the best use of funds to create healthy growth?" If there is a constant focus on being able to answer this simple question, VIA will remain a vibrant agency. Every business fulfills this purpose somehow—if a company doesn't create meaningful value for customers, the future of the business will be precarious.

Every time a client hires a service company for help, or a customer buys a product from a brand, it is an enormous act of trust. If we treat the money we receive simply as payment for goods and services rendered to our clients, we will feel fine just delivering what's expected. That's not good enough for VIA, and it shouldn't be for any company. Instead, we must make a commitment to deliver beyond expectations. Then, to constantly exceed our clients' expectations we will have to treat their money like our own money, remembering to always ask ourselves, "What if the money being tossed around by our clients belonged to us?" That will be the best guide for deciding how to invest the money we've been entrusted with when it comes to developing and delivering exceptional products and services.

I have to do this with all the investments I make in VIA, but that's easy because it's my money. We started VIA with $4,000 and some old computer equipment. With a bias toward investing rather than spending, VIA has flourished and grown into a long-lasting and vital company. But how do we get this focus when it's for a client and not ourselves? It's an exercise in empathy; it takes consistent effort to remember to do what's best for clients, not just what's expected or what's easiest, or worse yet, what's self-serving.

This way of thinking has become ingrained at VIA through working with companies like Welch's®. Welch's is actually a co-op made up of 450 family-owned farms that grow Concord grapes. Years ago Brad Irwin, the CEO of Welch's, invited us to meet some of the farmers, tour their vineyards, talk with the workers and see all their children running around the barnyard. The method to his madness was to make sure we saw firsthand how many people depend on Welch's for their livelihoods. He believed that outstanding advertising could drive Welch's business, and he wanted to make sure VIA would be as motivated as possible to create brilliant work. Work that would get Welch's great story out into the world—for the important reason that if we didn't, lots of good people would suffer the consequences. Seeing the faces of the farmers' children as they ran around the vineyards was a great motivator for keeping us working hard night and day, reminding us to treat their money like our own.

Ultimately, we should maintain an investor's mentality in everything we do so that our efforts today will grow into resources that help those we care about—our clients and our families. Being on budget means always being thoughtful about using money to make things better: the products we make, the services we deliver or the ideas we champion. The money itself doesn't ensure that things will be better; the actions we take in service to others will deliver the really meaningful returns.

Know the Price of the Priceless

Things only have the value that we give them.
—Molière

Our goal as an agency is to be the most valuable partner to our clients. We want them to be irrationally loyal to us, and that will only come from our total dedication to their success. We never want to be hired because we are cheap; we want to be hired because we are the best value—by a mile.

Achieving that starts by showing our clients how we can make their brands more valuable. How do we make something valuable? We make it extremely useful. We make it exceptional. We make it scarce. We make it desirable. Value doesn't always equal price. It has more to do with the brand's attributes. To raise the value of a product or service, it pays to invest in all aspects of a brand. So it's important to understand that our usefulness to our clients is not based solely on the deliverables we hand over. Beyond specific ads or promotions, the ideas we provide to them can be invaluable—ideas that make their products better, build the reputations of their brands as a result of their positive actions, or make an offering so desirable that they run out of product because demand is so high.

We once tackled the fun assignment of helping Unilever develop a campaign in Canada to revive the Klondike® Bar, that famous square hunk of chocolate-and-ice-cream bliss wrapped in silver foil. Instead of just delivering an ad, Amos Goss, a VIA Creative Director at the time, had the brilliant idea to make the historically square-shaped bars puck-shaped … and launch them during the NHL playoffs. Canada. Hockey. Guys. Ice cream. Pucks. It was a perfect storm of marketing brilliance. Needless to say, the Pucks flew off the shelves.

Many stores ran out of product, and shortly after the product was launched Klondike regained the No. 1 position in that market. A tasty accomplishment indeed.

We must be committed to finding ways to create meaningful value through the work we do. The future will belong to those who understand that the simple price of something won't drive an economy that will create a better standard of living for more people. It will take a more comprehensive definition of value to transform and evolve our socioeconomic systems, one that celebrates the good that is created in people's lives as a result of the things our efforts bring about. Asking ourselves how we can maximize the delta between the good and the harm we create is perhaps the new equation for the value of what we offer to the world. If we don't ask ourselves this question, the price we end up paying for our lack of caring could bankrupt us. But pushing to discover better ways of being will truly create priceless opportunities for us all.

Budgets Aren't Small, but Thinking Can Be

A blank cheque kills creativity.
—*Mokokoma Mokhonoana*

The old adage "You get what you pay for" can certainly be true, but I don't need to say much about the times when there is plenty of money available to accomplish the task at hand. It's the times when budgets are tight that challenge us all; however, the constraints of a small budget can liberate us because limited resources demand more innovative thinking and inventive ideas. The trend toward doing more with less will be with us as long as capitalism remains strong, so it pays to learn how to make one dollar work like five.

Limited funds can actually enhance creativity and resourcefulness, so we shouldn't use a low budget as an excuse for not being able to get the job done, a cry I have heard too often. Instead we should challenge ourselves to find new approaches, fresh methods and new ideas to reinvent the solution to a problem. I'm not saying clients should expect a Cadillac while paying for a Chevy, but perhaps we can teach them how to use public transportation well enough to never need a car again.

The best example of VIA stretching a dollar further didn't even use a dollar. The Salvation Army came to us for help in launching an advertising campaign to drive fundraising to support the organization's good work. However, there was no budget. Seriously. No money whatsoever. So, undaunted, a team of passionate VIA folks figured out a way to launch a campaign that cost "nothing." We handmade over 5,000 ads for a campaign telling the world that 83 percent of every dollar The Salvation Army earns goes to "Doing the Most Good." We stamped the message on pizza boxes and handwrote it on dirty car windshields, coffee sleeves, rocks, mirrors in public bathrooms—any free media we could get our mitts on. It was so successful that *Forbes* magazine said in a comment on the campaign, "If this idea isn't perfect, it's darn near it."

Don't Be Fair, Be Overly Fair

Real generosity toward the future lies in giving all to the present.
—*Albert Camus*

Early in VIA's history we landed a fixed-fee project with a large international technology company. We completed the work in much less time than we had estimated, so we returned 15 percent of the fixed fee to them. Our client was shocked because it was the first time a supplier had ever returned a portion of a fixed-fee contract. We kept that client for 10 years. The lesson: Being overly fair pays.

Profits are a sign of a healthy company. As VIA CFO Ivan Salazar likes to say, "Just because we like to make some money doesn't make us bad." When we are not making any profits, we can't reward people, invest in new capabilities or create reserves for the future. Strong profits are imperative. We should find clients who want us to make good money, sharing our belief that profits are required for the health of an exceptional agency. However, it's possible to be too focused on profits at the expense of giving great value to clients or working people too hard and burning them out. The key is finding the balance where it all works—where fairness is felt roughly equally by all parties. It's useful to consistently ask those we have monetary dealings with if they feel the shared economic relationship is fair on both sides—it tends to result in long-lasting relationships.

Being overly fair obviously extends to issues beyond those related to money. It speaks to being generous. To being magnanimous in victory. To taking on responsibilities that aren't necessarily our obligation but need to be taken care of, like offering to do the dishes once in a while even if we cooked the meal. It speaks to being the role model who always takes the high road, even when it would be easy to wallow in the mud. Someone's got to set the standard for a better way, and if we choose that role, we're unlikely to regret it.

Successful relationships are grounded in fairness. While negotiating to buy out one of VIA's wonderful creative founders, I was discussing the deal with a board member, Kip Moore, who had done over 100 business transactions in his career. He kept suggesting that we make a more generous counteroffer, exceeding what the departing partner had even asked for. The board member knew it was important for the person leaving to feel good about the deal. By being not just fair, but overly fair, we would be sure that my former partner—who was critical to the agency's history—would never feel taken advantage of. That was wise advice I often reflect on, and I have remained good friends with that partner I owe so much to even though he left years ago.

Of all the interesting people I've worked with at VIA over the years, my favorite is Cathy Robie, who was at the helm of our accounts receivable department for 20 years. And I make no bones about telling anyone at the agency that she's my favorite. Not because she always made sure we got paid (though I do love her for that). Or that I'd trust her with my life. But because she has constantly reminded me, throughout VIA's highs and lows—even during her own battle with cancer—of how lucky we are to be part of such a special group of free spirits; and that's what makes the money so important. To be on budget is essentially a reminder to stay on top of the things that enable us to get what we want out of life. Sometimes that means tending to the money that helps us achieve our goals and aspirations. But perhaps more importantly, it means understanding that the relationships and love we foster are much more valuable than the dollars and cents that often drive our actions.

7. Figure It Out

*If we all did the things we are really capable
of doing, we would literally astound ourselves.*
—*Thomas A. Edison*

At VIA, our creativity and work must help our clients grow their businesses. If our efforts don't increase sales or dramatically strengthen their brands' reputations, we are failing. The tricky thing about this challenge is that multiple variables go into moving the needle for a company: the product, the competitors' behavior, the audience's changing attitudes, the marketing trends,—damn, even the weather is a huge consideration when selling grapes or ski passes. It can feel mind-boggling.

So when facing formidable challenges, we have two choices: surrender or figure it out. I for one always vote for the latter, and that's what makes the job so much fun. (As an aside, it may seem like I am copping out on quote selection in this chapter because I have peppered it with sayings from just one person, the great American inventor, pacifist and businessman Thomas A. Edison. But he and I agree on so many elements of the "Figure it out" principle that I just had to. For example, he once said, "I never did a day's work in my life. It was all fun." I couldn't agree more.)

Here's the first step to figuring stuff out: Stop talking about why you can't do something. Complaining is unattractive and leads nowhere. Plus it's bad for your health, or at least my health, because I want to die when I am around complainers. The best thing I learned from my engineering days is that with a little will, you can figure anything out.

Persistence, the Unsexy Cousin of Creativity, Rules

*When you have exhausted all possibilities,
remember this—you haven't.*
—*Thomas A. Edison*

I was recently asked, "What is the most important attribute of an entrepreneur?" I immediately answered, "Creativity, followed by the second most important characteristic, persistence." The "Figure it out" principle, founded in a mashup of creativity and persistence, is the absolute motto of the entrepreneur, because when starting a venture, not a day goes by without facing some completely new challenge, and often we are on our own, so we get good at just figuring it out. This principle doesn't mean we should insulate ourselves when wrestling with questions and problems, and try to solve things by ourselves. Part of figuring it out is being enterprising enough to reach out to people or resources that can help us accomplish our new task. Even Edison needed some help along the way, calling himself more of a "sponge" than an inventor because he assimilated the thinking of so many others. We just need to continuously reach out in any direction necessary to figure it out. It works. I can think of hundreds of positive things that have been accomplished by the agency simply because of our "never give up" attitude.

VIA started with one anchor client, global electrical engineering company ABB. Our first priority as a new business was to diversify from 100 percent dependence on a single client and get client No. 2. This was intimidating because we had no history, no case studies, no references and no track record for new prospects to assess while considering whether to hire us. I targeted a few companies working in industries where I thought I could leverage a modicum of knowledge. One was Fraser Papers, headquartered in Connecticut. I persistently called the head of sales and marketing for four months, only to have him tell me that the real contact was another person, Sally Dean Lowe. I pursued her for the next three months until I landed a meeting, only to find out that her needs were different than her boss had told me. Then I had to persuade her to let me return in a couple of weeks with a completely different presentation. I finally convinced her that we could do the work, but because she was so busy and had so many other agency relationships, I had to politely pester her for another three months before we got our first assignment. Once we got in the door, we worked our magic, and Fraser became a multimillion-dollar anchor client for the next five years. I cannot overemphasize the gratitude I have for Sally's belief in VIA, and the importance of persistence. VIA wouldn't exist if not for a huge dose of it.

So when at a loss for exactly what to do next, do inexactly something.

Et Tu, Collaboration?

To do much clear thinking a person must arrange
for regular periods of solitude when they can concentrate
and indulge the imagination without distraction.
—*Thomas A. Edison*

VIA's culture errs on the side of collaboration because, as I've said earlier, that is the best approach for solving complex problems. That said, there is such a thing as too much collaboration. Shun large, long, unfocused meetings. Keep true contributors involved, not extras along for the ride. Favor action over deliberation. These practices focus collaboration on the need to solve problems and deliver results.

At other times we may need to be left to our own thoughts and cleverness—to leave the safety of the group, close the door, shut our computers off and think. If there's one insidious underbelly to the explosion of connected technology, it's that it erodes the quiet time for individual deliberation and contemplation. I still believe some of the best ideas are born from one individual deeply engrossed in contemplating bold, even radical solutions. Inviting too much groupthink can kill new ideas. We should be wary of this close friend called collaboration, and know when it's time to make our own way.

When do we know there's too much collaborating? When the conference room starts to stink as much as the ideas being generated from the group. Raise the flag and send everyone out to explore their own thoughts and solutions. By breaking up the groupthink, we stand a chance of finding fresh material. My favorite ritual for breaking up my day is to grab a pad of paper and a pencil (no computer; it's just a digital shackle that won't free our minds), go next door to the pub, sit in the back corner, order a bowl of chili (maybe even a beer) and just sit there and think. And sketch. And plot. And daydream. All by myself, ignoring everyone in the bar. It's by far the most productive time of my day. I highly recommend finding our own little escapes into the land of reflection and dreaming. It's good for our health and our work. Plus, when we go back to the office, we will usually have something tastier to share with our team than we did before lunch.

That approach saved us from canceling Christmas one year. We had been working hard on a new image campaign for a brilliant and extremely demanding client, David Goodman. Practically everyone at the agency was involved because we were all excited about the opportunity and wanted to do our best work yet. However, hyper-collaboration took over, and we just kept missing the mark. We had a lot of great stuff but nothing over the top. It was the week before Christmas, and the client wasn't feeling it, so he hopped on a plane and flew to our office.

Our huge team met with him, grinding away for two days, but nothing clicked. We just seemed to be over-kneading the dough. So at 10 the second night I told everyone to scatter: Go outside, go to your own office, go home—go to a dance club for all I care. Whatever. Just get the hell out and reflect. At the stroke of midnight, Chief Creative Officer Greg Smith came back to the conference table with an image of Iggy Pop doing a ridiculously extreme backbend and proclaimed that he had the idea for the new campaign. The client loved the new concept, and the work went on to win our first Effie for effectiveness and creativity. Happily, Christmas was saved; God bless everyone, especially Mr. Pop.

FACT OVER FICTION

Negative results are just what I want. They're just as valuable to me as positive results. I can never find the thing that does the job best until I find the ones that don't.
—*Thomas A. Edison*

Today's era of exploding data has transformed the way we solve problems. Despite that, people often try to pass off their opinions as facts when thinking through issues. The most powerful contributors to the business community in the future will be well served by a deep respect and appreciation for the analytical skills needed to assess what the data and facts are really telling us. Everyone in business, politics and society at large will need to become more adept at finding the stories buried within the mountains of information. That's the secret, not to leave storytelling behind but to become a better storyteller—one who has seen the truth through good and bad outcomes in the real world, and can translate it into the most compelling and powerful strategies to encourage people's behavior in better directions.

While navigating this era of data overload, VIA has been blessed with the leadership of Chief Strategy Officer David Burfeind. There is no better analytical storyteller in the business, a master of weaving data and dreams into the smartest strategies perfectly tailored to a specific company's opportunities—no matter how daunting its position.

And this was never better displayed than when we helped our valued client TD Banknorth break into the toughest, most competitive and oversaturated financial services market in the world: greater New York City. On every corner in that market was a branch, ATM or advertisement from one of the global powerhouse banks, and those competitors were spending hundreds of millions of dollars in marketing to carve out their small pieces of the pie. It was truly a David versus Goliath situation for our client. But by studying the data, which revealed the habits and desires of that commuter-based region, our David found the right stone for the battle.

Luckily, we were lined up to present our idea to two of the best client representatives we could ever ask for: Bill Ryan, TD Banknorth's CEO, and Tom Dyck, the CMO. But they were bankers, after all, not a breed known for risk taking. David began by asking, "What if we could use your competitors' biggest strength to fix your biggest weakness; win praise from your customers by relieving their biggest pain point; solve your distribution problems overnight; and immediately create huge buzz, credibility and awareness in the press while sticking it to the competition by offering something they couldn't beat and could only hope to match?" Needless to say, he had their attention with what sounded like a silver bullet. Then he shared the idea: "You will be the first bank to offer completely FREE ATM transactions."

Well, it's important to know that ATM fees are the opiate of choice for bankers—they are addicted to those fees. So as you can imagine, evidence of queasy feelings crossed their faces as we suggested that they forgo millions of dollars in ATM fees. But that's when David worked his most spellbinding magic. He mathematically proved that by essentially turning every one of their competitors' countless ATMs in the greater NYC area into TD Banknorth's own by waiving fees, they would save enough money on capital build-out and earn enough on new account openings to surpass the loss in ATM fees. Of course the way to bankers' hearts is through their wallets, and they gave the idea the green light.

The campaign was a great success for the bank, but the best reward for me came years later at a conference roundtable filled with CMOs, including many who had run the marketing efforts for the large banking competitors we went up against. The facilitator asked them to describe the most disruptive campaign they had ever dealt with, and one mentioned our Free ATM campaign. Then a couple more CMOs chimed in, remembering that move. I could tell by their faces what a pain we had created for them, and it seemed like they couldn't believe that such a small competitor could make so much trouble. That's the power we can mine from data. Because there is so much access to information today for all players, big and small, it can be the single most effective weapon we have in figuring things out.

We are living in a world that too often abdicates the responsibility to respect the facts and data defining our objective truths. As a result we allow mistruths to blind us, or break down the faith we have in our institutions. These lies create a fog of a war that is won by people in power who only care about themselves. When we abandon facts, we let in the opportunity for insidious actions and outcomes to flourish. We must dedicate ourselves to educating and advocating for a shared and factual truth. Only then do we stand a hope of finding solutions that would create the greatest good in the world.

Fail Forward

I have not failed. I've just found 10,000 ways that won't work.
—*Thomas A. Edison*

During my first career as an engineer I learned a technique called rapid prototyping, basically a design methodology that privileges the empirical data gathered from building and testing something quickly and, more importantly, watching it fail in order to reiterate and evolve as soon as possible. That method has stayed with me throughout my career in marketing. The fact is, everyone fails, especially when trying to do new things. The trick is to learn how to fail in a way that advances us—and not be so afraid to fail that we do nothing.

Whenever possible, it helps if we interject a "test and learn" mentality into the groups we're part of and the programs we're deploying. Fear of failure is the biggest threat to figuring out complex problems. If we are afraid to fail, we try nothing new; and before we know it, we become irrelevant. It's imperative to be able to learn from our mistakes and use the experience to quickly take a better idea to the table on the next round, before the failure takes us out of the game completely. That's why failing forward is important. We need to come back with a better answer before anyone catches on to us.

We all make mistakes. I could fill books with all the mistakes I've made. Some people can forget mistakes entirely, just block them out and move on, but I can't. I find that I sleep better when I just own up to my shortcomings. I don't beat myself up endlessly over missteps, but I do try to understand why they happened, and I commit to trying to avoid similar outcomes in the future. Don't get me wrong. I have repeated some mistakes. One of the biggest series of mistakes I made was opening, and subsequently closing, five—yes, five—other VIA offices. At different times we had offices in New York City, Boston, San Francisco, Zurich and Columbus. Call me a slow learner, but at least I learned. I learned a great deal from needing to close those offices, but the experience of opening them in such diverse places taught me a lot too. I met and was inspired by many employees and clients I worked with in each location. And I gathered endless great stories and memories from my escapades in figuring out how to survive in such a wide range of cultures (Zurich, Switzerland, is not San Francisco, California).

I lost a lot of money throughout this retraction, and sadly those failures affected many people I cared about deeply. Still, it's crucial to make sure we don't let our failures keep us from trying again. All those lessons have made me a little wiser but no less open to trying new things. That's the key: Instead of letting failure make us too cautious we can let failure make us more intelligently fearless.

And Now for Something Completely Different …

To invent, you need a good imagination and a pile of junk.
—*Thomas A. Edison*

On countless occasions I've been completely stuck in a problem because I've been too narrowly focused or too influenced by my first ideas. While many brainstorming techniques can enhance problem-solving and ideation, the simplest perhaps is to ask ourselves, "What's the 180 move here?" The complete turnaround. We've been traveling east all day, so let's turn around and head west for a bit. Ask ourselves what a completely different approach might look like, even if it's nonsensical or dramatically impractical. When we ask ourselves this question it often sheds light on a path that will lead from our safe, small thinking to something new, brighter and better.

My favorite example of this comes from another time we were working with TD Bank, an organization based in northern New England that was breaking into the very competitive Boston market. By employing traditional advertising methods, there was no way we could outspend the larger banks in the region. They had budgets much larger, plus established client bases and reputations. It seemed a daunting task, but we had to figure out something that would have impact, so we first set our minds on creating a solid new ad campaign. But we were worried that wouldn't be dramatic enough. While we were discussing the situation in the halls of the agency, a strategist not associated with the account, Jason Wright, happened to overhear us and lobbed in an unexpected idea.

Years before, the much beloved Boston Garden had been renamed the Fleet Center, after a financial services company that had since merged with another entity and disappeared. Jason suggested that we give the Garden back to New England by somehow wrangling the naming rights away from the current owner and changing back to the old name. That 180 idea completely shifted our thinking and approach. Through some remarkable late-night hustling and negotiations, we managed to secure the naming rights out from under several much larger suitors. The bank's generous act of renaming the Fleet Center the TD Garden touched the heartstrings of every hard-core Celtics and Bruins fan (that is, everyone in New England). Four months later, the bank's awareness had gone from single digits to 70 percent in the marketplace with essentially no advertising—a nearly unheard of accomplishment.

Different is good. Yet it can be uncomfortable to express another point of view or share a contrarian idea. Being different from the crowd can generate fear of judgment or alienation. But we should fight for different. Fight for the oddball. Fight for things that have never been done before. If we are lucky enough to come across an idea with potential that has never before been attempted, we should find the courage to give it a try. New ways of solving complex problems almost always require new ways of thinking and different ways of acting.

The most meaningful and influential book I ever read was the biography of Mahatma Gandhi, the primary leader of India's independence movement. That slight man faced down the power of the British Empire by spinning cloth and making salt. His pacifist ways were different almost to the point of being laughable. Yet never has there been a more brilliant, inventive and effective modern leader, to me, than Gandhi. He proved that when we completely commit to figuring it out, doing the impossible doesn't seem that difficult.

8. Find the Magic

Whatever you can do or dream you can, begin it.
For boldness has genius, power and magic in it.
—Johann Wolfgang von Goethe

One of VIA's founders, Rich Rico, could often be seen in his office with his back to the door, hunched over his computer mumbling to himself. Much like a mantra, he'd say the same words over and over. Then when you got closer, you could hear that he was quietly chanting, "Find the magic, find the magic, find the magic." Rich was a driven copywriter who would spend hours and hours on the hunt for the perfect turn of phrase, the right name for a new product, or a big idea. He was correct that time is not the only thing we need to create something amazing. We need a little magic.

VIA's whole strategy can be summed up by the equation Creativity > Creative. Yes, our output, called the creative in the ad world, is indispensable. But we can all achieve some measure of greatness by bringing creativity to every aspect of our work. We need the creativity of every single person at VIA to find new and better ways of running the agency and delivering brilliant work to our clients. One of my primary beliefs is that creativity is a basic human need. Much like we need to eat or have sex, we need to be creative. Everyone does.

Sadly, too many people deny themselves the pleasure of creating. I can't tell you the number of times I have heard people say, "I'm just not creative." That's not true. Our humanity is defined by the fact that we can create. The problem is that the world doesn't always define creativity broadly enough. Or recognize this basic need to ensure that everyone gets an opportunity to be creative. At VIA we are all expected to contribute our best ideas, everyone's contribution is valued, and we try to apply creativity to every corner of our business (except our accounting practices, of course).

One of my assistants, Crista Cruz Crum, had a remarkable talent for gift giving. She could find just the right selection of items and arrange them in a beautiful, one-of-a-kind creation that was just perfect for the recipient. Every time she sent one of her gifts to a prospective client I got a gushing thank-you note, and often it was the reason the client would take my call, allowing me to explore ways of working together. Her creativity helped VIA grow.

Where do new ideas come from? New ways of seeing the world? Better ways of doing things? Beautifully crafted works? There is wonderful mystery to the creative exploration of life. It's hard to fabricate a foolproof method for finding genius. Creativity is too fickle and coy to be programmed into some fail-safe system for the production of the truly new. That said, here are a few tricks to help find the magic more often.

Let It Flow

Dogs have boundless enthusiasm but no sense of shame. I should have a dog as a life coach.
—Moby

Mihály Csíkszentmihályi, a leading thinker in positive psychology, coined the term *flow* for "the mental state of operation in which a person performing an activity is fully immersed in a feeling of energized focus, full involvement, and enjoyment in the process of the activity. In essence, flow is characterized by complete absorption in what one does" (*Wikipedia, The Free Encyclopedia*, s.v. "Flow," accessed December 8, 2015, https://en.wikipedia.org/wiki/ Flow_%28psychology%29). A real and hugely desirable state of being, flow can be discovered in many different aspects of life, both at work and at home. It's easiest for me to find flow when I am in my studio making art. I experience a feeling of deep contentment almost immediately, and the rest of the world disappears. I have felt this at work also—usually when dealing with people I trust and enjoy, and doing the things I love most. The better the flow, the greater the creativity. But flow is not easy to find. I think it helps to stack the deck to reach that state of mind.

For example:

Know what you love
We all have to do things we don't like to do. That's life. But be honest with yourself, really honest, in acknowledging the things you love to do. Don't listen to others in this pursuit; trust your gut. If you discover the threads that lead to your passions, you can start working toward filling your life with those activities. It can take a long time and even some plotting to get enough of the things you love into your job or life, but you will never get there if you aren't honest about what you love. I started my career in engineering, but I knew I would find marketing more inspiring. It took me eight years to get into a position where I was working in marketing every day. When that happened I experienced more flow in one week at VIA than I had managed to muster in an entire year as an engineer. And it's never too late. I was around 50 by the time I realized I was ready to make my art.

Set your stage
When I was in high school an exchange student named Matteo Orsingher taught me a few songs on the guitar. But as life went on, marriage, kids and work became my priorities, and the guitar got relegated to the back of the closet and forgotten. Then years later that same friend gave me the best advice I ever got regarding my playing. "Pull it out and leave it hanging," he said. (Did I mention he was Italian?) Well, that is just what I did. By taking my guitar out of the closet and hanging it on the wall in the living room I could grab it easily, so I started playing every day, even if it was just one song, and that has transformed my playing and given me thousands of small moments of flow. Do the same in your world. Make the time to set up your life so it's focused on the things most important to you. Organize your environment so you have access to the things you

love best. If you're disciplined about getting the necessary mundane tasks out of the way efficiently, you'll have more time to pursue what really matters.

Begin anywhere
The genius contemporary composer and thinker John Cage once gave this amazing piece of advice: "Begin anywhere." Like inertia, creative block is real and mysterious. Sometimes I find large, complex tasks overwhelming; it's hard to know where to begin. So learn to begin anywhere. For me starting is the hardest part, but once the flow breaks through a mental block, it just keeps rolling. Don't judge what comes out of you at the beginning. Don't self-edit (plenty of time for that later). As Marcel Duchamp said, "In a word, do less self-analysis and enjoy your work without worrying about opinions, your own as well as others." Just let the ideas, scribbles, words and music come pouring out. It's like priming a pump. You just need a few cups to start the water flowing.

Anyone can make a commitment to finding flow. A few years ago our client Welch's had a sadly underused mascot called Welchy, a huge jar of grape jelly with a big smile and googly eyes. Welchy was limited to making random appearances at company picnics and occasional store visits, but Amos Goss, then a copywriter at VIA, saw a big opportunity. Matching his passion for performance with his love of the client's brand, he came up with an idea he wanted to present to the Welch's team during their next agency visit—and he asked that it be kept a secret from both the client and me.

The day arrived, and as we were wrapping up the meeting I heard a thundering rendition of the infectious song "Peanut Butter Jelly Time" kick in over the conference room sound system. Amos, dressed in the Welchy costume, burst into the room and started performing some of the most classic junior high dance moves on the planet: the "Galloping Cowboy with a Lasso," the "Groggy Gorilla" and my personal favorite, "Your Mom Playing Video Games." This went on for seven hilarious minutes. When the music stopped he lifted off his purple headpiece, revealing his smiling face for the first time. Then he excitedly explained how he wanted to do those dances on the Jumbotron during halftime shows at Celtics games, and how we could do a tie-in with Kevin Garnett, the team center, who ate a PB&J before every game. Then he stopped and looked inquisitively at us because we were all staring at him in shock. You see, Amos was so in the flow that he didn't realize blood was streaming down his face. The headpiece was a bit small, and it had been smashing into his nose during his wild dancing, causing it to erupt.

Talk about suffering for your art. But it was all worth it, as he was thrilled when the client approved the idea and sent him to TD Garden to do his thing. Watching Amos, dressed as Welchy, on the Jumbotron leading thousands of fans in the "Funky Chicken" may just have been the most magical moment in VIA's history.

Screw Around More

When you make music or write or create, it's really your job to have mind-blowing, irresponsible, condomless sex with whatever idea it is you're writing about at the time.
—*Lady Gaga*

When was the last time you heard of anyone getting a genius idea while sitting in the office, staring at a computer screen, constantly being interrupted by his or her smartphone? Ah, I think that might be never. Ideas most often sneak up on us. While on a jog in the woods. While playing with our children. During walks with our dogs. I think when the mind disengages from worrying, or even thinking about anything at all, surprises arise. The trick is to learn to play and explore more. Relax into a state that opens the mind.

Some of the most interesting things I have created began with a mindless act like picking up a random object and trying to find a way it might relate to the problem at hand. Really, any object will do. I am always amazed at how the mind will find connections. As the body needs to breathe, the mind needs to link. When we throw ourselves off track and venture into a non sequitur with eyes wide open, surprises appear. It's great to experiment with random acts of body and mind, and feel what comes up. When we feel stuck, we should go outside. Go to used bookstores. Thrift stores. Markets. The woods. The grocery store. The beach. The basement. The library. The dump. When our minds take in our surroundings, they start putting together the links we need to get back to solving our challenges in a completely new and inventive way.

In our first office in an old molasses factory on Portland's Danforth Street we had a pingpong table. People played all hours of the day and night. Good players. Bad players. Everyone spent time at the table. I bet many corporate cultures would view that as a complete assault on productivity. Or at the other end of the spectrum, a few companies might have something like a pingpong table mainly for show. For us, it was a sacred place. Yes, people would talk smack about each other's game, but they also talked about literature. Music. Problems they had with raising their kids. Or a block they were having in tackling a client assignment. I discovered that more good ideas came from time at the pingpong table than the conference rooms.

When we moved into the Baxter Building, Teddy Stoecklein, then a Creative Director at VIA, realized we had no room for the pingpong table. So with his own two hands, and the hands of a few other VIA faithful, he carried in yards of crushed oyster shells to build a bocce court in the open courtyard at the center of our building. Yes, so he could have a reason to screw around during work hours. And that is the whole point.

Our Ideas vs. My Ideas

*The worst thing you can think
about when you're working is yourself.*
—Agnes Martin

Collaborative creativity, not self-expression, powers most businesses. If you want to be an artist or explore your own specific point of view on things, there is nothing I would applaud more; just don't do it on company time. Organizations and corporations exist to serve a collective need. Collaboration is the engine of these entities. So it's important to understand that ideas developed within companies are different; they exist to serve the greater good of all employees and clients, as well as their communities.

It can be a difficult and emotional balancing act for many individuals to learn how to contribute their talents and thinking in a way that doesn't feel demeaning to their creative integrity. We are all sensitive to how our ideas are treated; it's just human nature. So organizations have to learn how to let people share their best thinking, mix it with other people's best thinking and ensure that the strongest ideas reach their fullest potential. That is no easy task. And it calls for some magic. So here are some guidelines for developing the best ideas:

It's everyone's idea

I try to use the royal "we" whenever I talk about the ideas created by the agency, because like the queen, when I talk about the work we do, I fully understand that everyone in VIA's realm helped create it. I even avoid singling out the team that led the development of a campaign when speaking publicly because I always forget to mention someone. Always. And the fact is, I would have to name everyone at the agency every time I tried to recognize people because it is the absolute truth that no matter how small the part, our success is only realized through everyone's contributions.

Criticize constructively

Yes, the work can be stupid but never the people behind the work. I think there are good and bad ways to give criticism about the work we all make. Our ideas float around the agency and take on lives of their own. Once they come to life, we should all try to find ways to help them grow. Constructive criticism can become the most valuable fertilizer within the organization, and offering excellent criticism is a skill people can develop. For example:

- Direct your comments toward the idea, not the person.
- Ask questions instead of assuming your interpretations of the idea are complete.
- Be specific in your feedback.
- Try to contribute to the betterment of the idea versus simply stating what is wrong with it.

No matter how confident a person may be, it takes great courage to share ideas and work with others. We should always aim to be kind and deeply respectful with our comments about someone's work. Crapping on another's efforts in an unconstructive way seems to be the strength of the most miserable people in most companies. Better to be the horse that pulls the work forward, not the ass that stays stuck in the mud.

Lose your attachments
Buddha said, "The root of suffering is attachment." Surprisingly, this applies readily to collaborative ideation. The more a person clings to "my idea," the harder it is to see input that could improve the idea. I'm not saying that we should give up on our ideas if we think they're the best ones; just that putting our egos aside will allow us to know for sure. And, trust me, doing that will reduce our suffering as well as the suffering of those around us.

An organization that zealously and collaboratively develops the best ideas, wherever they come from, will be unstoppable. A classic example of embracing "our idea" came when we were producing VIA's very first TV spot. It was for an online brokerage firm called BrownCo, a division of J.P. Morgan Chase & Co., and we were under lots of pressure to prove that we could do high-end broadcast TV. We were confident, but we knew it would take many great people and new ideas and thinking to pull it off.

With that in mind, the first thing Chief Creative Officer Greg Smith did was hire the best agency producer in the business, Mary Hanifin. Sometimes finding the magic starts with finding the right person for the job, and Mary was the right person, having done classic spots for Volkswagen®, Cadillac and the Gap®.

But the story doesn't end there. As it turns out, Mary was able to coax Academy Award–winning director Errol Morris to bid on the job. That was indeed a coup, with one possible exception: He was known to be a mad perfectionist with a reputation for "going rogue" if he felt the work was not heading in a direction he favored. In fact, he had just finished creating a brilliant campaign for Apple, during which he and Steve Jobs were said to have had some legendary battles about creative direction. These facts made our client nervous. Up until the final hour of bidding the job, it looked as though we would pass on Errol and opt for a serviceable, though less-than-spectacular, bid from our No. 2 director.

That was until Greg, Mary and Ron Clayton, the lead copywriter on the campaign, decided to rally the troops and make an impassioned plea for hiring Errol. They knew how rare it is to work with that type of genius, and while it may come with challenges, we don't walk away from the potential for something magical to happen that working with unique talent offers. So those three put their reputations on the line and convinced the client to award the production to Errol and his team.

To be honest, it started out a little rocky. About four hours into the first day of casting, Errol became frustrated that none of the actors up to that point had given a good read. He immediately began addressing what he felt might be issues with the script, expressing disgust particularly with the seemingly innocuous line, "It takes serious tools to make serious investments." Finally Errol just erupted: "I mean SERIOUS TOOLS? Are you kidding me? SERIOUS TOOLS? WHAT IS A SERIOUS TOOL ANYWAY?"

The room fell silent. The client and our team of creatives, producers and strategists looked on, uncertain how to respond. I remember thinking, "Well, this could be the first and last TV shoot we ever do."

Then Greg decided to chime in on the matter, stating, "I'd say a serious tool could be anything from a real-time capital gains tracker to an egomaniacal Oscar-winning director."

Mary's eyes widened. Ron's jaw dropped.

Errol was another matter. At first, he winced when he heard the comment, and it seemed to take a good 30 seconds for him to fully comprehend what Greg had just said. But when he did, his face scrunched into a wide smile, and he shouted with glee, "THAT'S GOOD. THAT'S GOOD. THAT'S A GOOD ONE."

With that, the casting director called, "Next," and the team never looked back. The shoot was a great success, and Errol brought his distinct form of genius and intellectual curiosity to a project that would've simply been *good* without him. In the end this experience underscores the need to put egos aside and trust in the talents and contributions of the entire team, for that is the best way to make things turn out truly magical.

To Be or Not to Be

Sometimes the road less traveled is less traveled for a reason.
—Jerry Seinfeld

What's the difference between a great idea and a not-so-great idea? The funny thing is that it costs the same to come up with a lousy idea as a good idea, so money doesn't really determine the difference in most cases. Until the ideas are executed and tested in the wild, it's often hard to tell which ideas are best. But knowing which ideas to protect and which to kill can often be harder than generating the ideas in the first place.

Different kinds of ideas can typically be categorized. Recognizing the category each idea fits into will help us determine which ones should be killed and which should be cultivated. Obviously, if the idea we're considering doesn't address the problem we were asked to solve, we must kill it. But here are some other typical types of ideas worth learning to identify on our path to becoming better creators of all things awesome.

The "first" idea
Our first ideas are most often clichéd, obvious or less than magical. So we should get them out of our system fast and kill them. Occasionally, our very first idea was the right idea, but we can dig it out of the trash later if that turns out to be the case.

The "my" idea
We're all human, and often we fall so completely in love with our own ideas they blind us. People never think their own children are ugly. We should always be our harshest critic. We can cultivate objectivity in our self-criticism by asking ourselves, "Would I love this idea if someone else had created it?" If the answer is maybe not, it's best to kill the idea.

The "undersold" idea
Shame on us if we don't learn to sell our ideas or protect others' great ideas. I have seen many wonderful ideas fail to be developed because people couldn't convey their power. To sell a great idea, we should first tell how it will solve the problem at hand, then explain why it is right or unique for the specific situation, and finally describe how it will be so brilliantly executed that all who bear witness will shed tears of joy. If we do it with passion and sincerity, we may even sell a few average ideas now and then.

The "ugly duckling" idea
Let's face it; we've all been in a meeting when someone lays a turd of an idea. It sounds so dumb when first uttered that the entire room recoils in an effort to escape the stink. I have learned to take special notice when this happens. Whenever I observe a big reaction, even if it seems negative, there might be something great within. It's wise to protect the idea for a while so that the groupthink doesn't immediately reject it. Beware of conventional wisdom; it sometimes exists to smother unconventional genius.

The "scary" idea

"An idea that is not dangerous is unworthy of being called an idea at all," Oscar Wilde once quipped. Really scary ideas meet constant opposition because most people don't have the risk tolerance for them. But those never-done-before ideas can be game changers. And big ideas are almost always scary on some level. To tackle scary ideas we need to be brave. So we should cultivate the courage in ourselves and those around us to try to do the impossible. By addressing fears head-on, we can make obstacles seem a bit smaller and the opportunity for real glory that much bigger.

The "right" idea

I get sick of listening to people blather on about big ideas. Many small ideas are treated like big ideas by people who don't know the difference. Or people try to romanticize the big idea to obfuscate the fact that not everything needs to get solved with big ideas. Though it clearly has its place in the world, the big idea is not needed for every situation. I prefer to develop the skills to find the right idea. The right idea solves the problem at hand with utmost elegance, simplicity, cleverness and efficiency. Right ideas get as close to perfection as an idea can. Sometimes right ideas can be big ideas, but just as often they are small, perfectly crafted ideas just right enough to bring about the desired change. Ask Rosa Parks, Jane Goodall or Gandhi. All determined the simple act of sitting peacefully to be the right idea. And each changed the world.

A Case for Crafting Magical Work

*Design is not making beauty, beauty emerges
from selection, affinities, integration, love.*
—Louis Kahn

I use the word *magical* here instead of *beautiful*, but beauty in the magical sense is perhaps what I mean. Because *beauty* has too many cultural, political and social complexities, *magical*—which has an unknowable element of being just so—will have to do. I deeply believe the world needs to strive to create awe and wonder. It goes back to my belief that creativity is a human need. We are sustained by encountering acts of humankind that inspire, entertain and mesmerize us.

It's not always necessary to make things beautiful, or magical. But whenever and wherever we can bring magic into the world through our work, we add a richness that makes life much more rewarding and interesting. It's the difference between the Brooklyn Bridge and the Queensboro Bridge. The Guggenheim Museum building and the New Museum building. Bruce Springsteen's "Thunder Road" and the Spice Girls' "Wannabe." Both songs are about trying to woo a lover—needless to say, I think, one is dramatically more magical.

Concocting this kind of magic takes a dedication to craft—our commitment to hone and care for the making of the ideas we dream up. Craft seems like a practice out of step with our technologically advanced times. But developing our skills as craftspeople is perhaps even more important if we are to continue to find the magic as technology takes over more and more human tasks. Though we use computers in making so many things today, human decision making around details large and small gives creators the power to push things to greatness. The attention, and even obsession, to make things the best they can be must be at the heart of all endeavors that hope to engage and move people. I like calling VIA a shop because it paints a picture of craftspeople laboring to build great things, which is noble work indeed.

When deciding to undertake a task with the potential to be special, even magical, we often meet with resistance. Pursuing unconventional or risky opportunities requires a good dose of courage and conviction. But going for them is usually worth it. In 2009, during the throes of the Great Recession, I made a tough decision (against the advice of my board) to take over the dilapidated Baxter Building, built in 1888 as Portland's library, in hopes of resurrecting it into VIA's headquarters. Many people thought it was insane, but with the amazing craft and care of creative partners like architect Scott Simons, fine-arts furniture maker Jamie Johnston, and artists John and Linda Myers, plus countless talented carpenters, electricians and plumbers, we turned the Baxter Building into what I believe is one of the most inspiring workplaces in the world. My advice is to constantly be on the lookout for opportunities where you can make some magic happen. If you find one, pounce on it and pour your heart and soul into making it sparkle.

When we create work with a design, quality or character that makes us laugh, think, question, act, sing or feel a jolt of joy, we have done something real to make the world better. If we all share this mission to develop our creativity to its fullest, we could save the planet from the mistakes made by those unwilling to change. It is an honor to work in a business that celebrates creativity so enthusiastically. We should never take lightly the efforts needed to cultivate our gifts to find the magic. The Roman poet Ovid said, "Beauty is a fragile gift." Use your gift well.

9. Do Work That Makes You Proud

I am overly ambitious, because I realize it can be done.
—Pharrell Williams

Early in my career I was assigned the design of a fairly significant engineering project—when I was a college intern at a nuclear plant, no less. No pressure there. Because engineering is a very creative profession, there are usually several ways to solve any problem. I worked on the project for about a week before asking to present my design to my manager. I prepped for the presentation, walked into his office and was just about to begin when he asked me one simple question, "Are you proud of your work?" I was stopped cold, thrown off track from my rehearsed pitch. "Was I proud?" I remember thinking. "Was that the very best I could do?" The answer that bubbled up was no. I could do better. So I asked, "Could I have another week?"

My boss knew I would be the toughest critic of my own work if I stopped to think about it. Doing work that makes you proud usually means you've worked just about as hard as you could and there is little more you could do. That's about the best we can ask of people. Did they make their absolute best effort? This principle is a reminder to never just mail in our work. Make it the best we possibly can. Always aim to outdo our best efforts, which will create a deep sense of pride for us, not a hollow or arrogant one.

The World Should Be Like Gertrude Stein's Living Room

I love my family, even as I critique their dysfunctionalities.
—bell hooks

"Do work that makes you proud" is the quality standard at VIA. If we can say with all honesty and conviction that we are proud of the work we have produced, I bet it is pretty good work. But obviously, much is involved in turning good work into great work. It's important to develop a culture of rigorous dialogue about our work, our process, competitors' work, the philosophy guiding our work, social trends affecting the work and new techniques for doing the work. All of it. Cultivating an environment that challenges the work and the quality of its creation ensures constant evolution.

Rigorous and open dialogue should be the lifeblood of a place searching to do ever-greater things. I have always tried to find ways to create interesting forums and interactions that help me see the work I do against a broader backdrop of the world. One way I have accomplished that is by bringing together people with diverse backgrounds and interests to engage them in topics within and beyond their areas of expertise. For years, I hosted the VIA Salon

Series in cities across the U.S. They were evenings in the spirit of Gertrude Stein's Paris life, filled with good questions, conversation, food, drink and music. The ensuing interactions usually opened our minds and hearts a bit, inspiring self-reflection and new perspectives. Plus they were always serious fun.

To foster even greater internal dialogue at VIA, I studied the work of physicist and philosopher David Bohm, who developed ideas about improving interpersonal communications to better understand how to solve complex problems. Called Bohmian Dialogue, his approach strives to create open dialogue so that everyone's feelings and opinions can be shared equally and nonjudgmentally. When people in a group understand others' points of view as fully as possible, better decision making naturally occurs. It doesn't mean people will change their beliefs or positions; just that awareness is increased, and stronger actions that fairly benefit the group as a whole can be taken.

Ideas that lead to better group awareness are instrumental for creating the best companies of tomorrow. At VIA, finding ways for everyone's voice to be heard makes the agency stronger. Being transparent with information and expectations builds a more trusting workplace. If we want to be creative, we have to establish deep trust so people can share their ideas free of attacks. These interactions work best face to face—hiding behind a digital veil all too often weakens real connection and empathy. To promote communication and increase awareness at VIA, we also maintain dialogue groups; participate in salon discussions; and host lecture series, bringing the top marketers and thinkers to the agency. Once a month we gather for Free Beer & Fiction, an evening when VIAns share theme-inspired fiction they've written along with a new beer and lots of good conversation. Anything that creates interaction and pushes learning is encouraged.

The bottom line is if we want to grow, we need to be in the know. Quality and excellence are pursuits, not destinations. But if we instigate rigorous, open dialogue around us and gain understanding that improves our work day after day, we can make everyone proud.

Give Away All the Credit

Leaders are best when people barely know
they exist, when their work is done, their aims
fulfilled, the people will say: we did it ourselves.
—Lao Tzu

Pride can be crippling and insidious. Our insecurities can get the better of us if we become too prideful, and if our egos become addicted to pride, we may try to take the credit for anything we are associated with. On the other hand, letting go of our egos can liberate and empower us to accomplish anything because it can help us harness the efforts of those we work with to reach their greatest potential, the goal of most leadership challenges.

Want to know the most valued secret of enlightened leaders? They happily give all the credit for success to others and willingly take the responsibility for failures themselves. If we learn to do this, we will eliminate much fear in the people we lead or manage. Giving them the chance to receive the rewards of any success they are part of will drive them to reach their greatest potential. Like him or not, longtime quarterback for the New England Patriots, Tom Brady, always attributes his success to his offensive line, his receivers and his special teams—everybody in his organization except himself. And when the Patriots lose, it's on his shoulders, and he usually says he should have played better. It's no coincidence that his teams have won more Super Bowls than any other in the history of the game.

This way of being is simple, and doesn't just apply to leaders; it applies to anyone working in a group. But time and time again we see people hoarding accolades or blaming others for their failures. It's important to have compassion for these kinds of people, as they often harbor deep unhappiness, and their insecurities drown out their better judgment. Sometimes we see people who take all the credit for themselves advance their careers on the backs of others' efforts, and that's hard to stomach. But in the long run, remember, good karma always seems to win.

Always Better Your Best

Don't bunt. Aim out of the ballpark.
Aim for the company of immortals.
—David Ogilvy

Perhaps the simplest trick I play to improve my work is to always ask myself two things: "Is my work different enough from other work I have seen?" and, "Is it the best work I have ever done?" If I do something that is no better than my past work, or is too similar to others' work, I know I haven't finished my task. I will continue working, if possible, until I make it better. Sometimes I run out of time and need to accept the results. But if we're always outdoing what we've done before, we will be pretty content with our work.

Another important aspect of "bettering your best" involves not just making *a* statement with your work but making *your* statement with your work. It's important for the essence of your work to be something you can always feel proud of, because it reflects the things you find meaningful. For example, Greenpeace approached us a few years ago and asked us to develop a campaign targeting giant server-farm operators like Apple, Google and Microsoft® and calling them on their use of dirty energy sources to power their facilities. We said we'd take the assignment, but we needed to do it in a constructive way that might actually inspire those companies to change their practices. A bomb-throwing approach didn't feel right to us. Greenpeace agreed and we made a series of funny, good-natured videos that named those big companies but in a creative way that invited them to switch to clean energy sources, which many then started doing.

That campaign was one of the most awarded in the agency's history. Trying to top that for the follow-up campaign the next year, we enlisted comedian, musician and avant-garde performer Reggie Watts to tell the story, and the new campaign was even better than the first. Be sure to make your statement and find ways to make it better. That way you'll probably never regret your work.

We want to avoid the trap of having to accept work we don't believe in. Years ago, while pitching our first national campaign to a food company, we presented two very strong campaigns and a third we were sure the client would kill. Well, the client loved the one we thought was a dog. And we were stuck with it—until Creative Director Ian Dunn helped us dodge that bullet with a genius modification to the campaign. Lucky for us! The takeaway: We should only present work we can be proud of. We will be judged on the worst work we put into the world, so we only want to give our best work a shot at seeing the light of day.

Anyone who has seen my office or taken a look at my computer knows I don't keep many old files or documents, and I rarely go back to the ones I have kept. My philosophy is if I created it once, I can do it better next time, so why keep it around? In the advertising business, we create way more ideas and campaigns than we ever use. I can honestly say, however, that we have never reused or revisited an old idea and sold it to a new client. We always start fresh because we will do better work to fit the new situation. That is the attitude of greatness: Next time we will do it even better.

CAN YOU HAVE TOO MANY PARTIES?

Beer is living proof that God loves us and wants us to be happy.
—Benjamin Franklin

When I decided it was time to hire my replacement as CEO, I knew I had the right person when I learned that she had a mirrored disco ball permanently hardwired in her family room. Among her many talents is Leeann Leahy's knack for throwing a great party. Not just because she loves to have a good time (which, by the way, she does) but also because she understands the importance of celebrating life through tradition, rituals and spontaneity. A life without celebration goes by unappreciated.

This applies on the job as well. We should show pride in our work by celebrating it. Celebrate our accomplishments. Celebrate commitment, loyalty and genius. Even celebrate our failures once in a while. People today work too hard. The promise of technology to make everyone's life easier doesn't seem to have materialized. Vacations are squeezed and interrupted endlessly by technological connectivity. People are working longer. Europe doesn't even shut down in August anymore. So sad.

We need to find ways to celebrate more. I wasn't very good at it in my early years of running VIA. Once we achieved some kind of success, I would push us on to the next goal, always worrying that at any day we could go out of business if we got arrogant or didn't work constantly. Then 9/11 happened. We had just made it through the internet bubble burst (barely) in the late 1990s when our world was rocked. Fortunately, we lost no one working in our New York office on the corner of Varick and Canal, but the ensuing fallout halted business, forcing us to close that location, and put us into some extremely difficult years of operation. It was a wake-up call. Everything is fragile, and most things are out of our control.
So we should celebrate while we can.

We have always had amazing holiday and summer parties—wild, fun and sentimental affairs—with awards like The VIA Way for the unsung heroes of the agency and the Schwartzmanship Award, an annual award (not always given) that recognizes someone who has gone above and beyond in serving clients and the agency. Plus, now we also take time to celebrate new client wins, years of service, people having babies, new dogs, birthdays, summer Fridays, life. Our "Go. Do." series—when we close the agency for an hour at lunch to dance at a local bar, have an impromptu snow sculpture competition or take over the local art museum—makes real our commitment to celebrating the hard work we do and getting inspired for the next round of creative pursuits coming our way.

In the immortal words of the great musician philosopher Prince, "But life is just a party, and parties weren't meant to last." So celebrate while you still can because it all slips by so quickly.

Pride of Ownership

Enough is better than too much.
—French Proverb

Concentration of wealth, I believe, is one of the leading indicators of a sick society. French Queen Marie Antoinette found that out the hard way. The Economic Policy Institute reported in 2014 that the average CEO salary for the country's 350 largest companies was 303 times that of the average worker's pay. Companies today should have more balanced compensation models. I think the best and fairest way to achieve collective greatness is to ensure that all members of a group, company or community participate in the success and failure of the entity, making sure that risk and reward are fairly and intelligently distributed. Plus, if everyone has skin in the game, people will be more committed and focused on driving success.

VIA has always shared profits, but in 2015 we embarked on a journey to turn the company into an employee-owned entity. In many indigenous cultures, people in the community who want more resources than they need are viewed as having some sort of mental illness. Why do we need more stuff than we can use? In preparation for the next phase of our lives, my wife, Linda, and I took a cue from that wisdom and decided the best thing to do rather than sell the agency would be to gradually turn ownership over to the employees. We hope this model will make VIA even greater while equitably sharing the wealth created through the entire team's efforts: If everyone contributes, everyone fairly benefits. Not equally but fairly, providing personal and collective motivation that we believe will ensure the longevity and sustainability of VIA for generations to come, and nothing would make us prouder.

As one way to address the challenges raised by the concentration of wealth, the elimination of human work by computer automation, and the systemic enablers of generational poverty, the idea of employee ownership should be explored and championed in more companies. But this is just one idea of many that need to be cultivated. Getting greater involvement in addressing the formidable challenges of our times is paramount. As employees, citizens and family members we must all become activists. The pride we can collectively achieve will only be realized when all are involved in our society in healthy and meaningful ways. As feminist writer and civil rights activist Audre Lorde once said, "I am not free while any woman is unfree, even when her shackles are very different from my own."

10. Believe

Never doubt that a small group of thoughtful, committed citizens can change the world; indeed, it's the only thing that ever has.
—Margaret Mead

Believing in something can be hard because it often requires accepting things that seem almost impossible. But I know, without hesitation, that one of the most powerful gifts we have is the ability to believe in the impossible. Nothing of merit has ever been accomplished without this gift. Landing on the moon. Curing polio. Ending segregation. All those things seemed ridiculous at one time to everyone but a few dedicated people who believed in the impossible.

Right before I started VIA many people told me I was on a fool's errand. How could an engineer who had never stepped foot in an ad agency start an international shop in Portland, Maine? To be fair, it did sound rather far-fetched when you put it that way. However, I had a deep belief in myself and the people who started the shop with me. I believed we were going to be successful. Every day, day after day, on and on, I kept believing. When we won our first piece of business, I believed. When I had to make payroll using my credit card, I believed. When we opened offices in New York, San Francisco and Boston, I believed. And when we had to close those offices, I still believed. Then in the summer of 2011, I was sitting in a hotel ballroom in Denver with Chief Creative Officer Greg Smith when Rupal Parekh, an editor from *Ad Age* magazine called out, "The VIA Agency." We had been selected from roughly 800 firms as the Ad Age Small Agency of the Year. I called my wife to tell her the great news and caught a plane home the next morning. When I told the agency, we cheered. Then we started focusing on becoming Agency of the Year, a goal I completely believe we will achieve one day.

Believing in something almost bigger than we can imagine helps inspire us. It can give purpose to our actions and meaning to our work. VIA's purpose has been unwavering since its founding: help clients grow through creativity. Our approach to fulfilling this purpose is grounded in our name, VIA, an acronym for Vision, Instinct and Action. In the highest sense, it is our process for approaching the work we do. Following those three words has helped guide us in doing the impossible—we simply needed to believe.

Imagining a Better Way: Vision, Instinct, Action

You can be anything you want to be, do anything you set out
to accomplish if you hold to that desire with singleness of purpose.
—Abraham Lincoln

VIA means "way" in Latin. At VIA we have always believed our mission is to find a better way. It starts with a clear vision. Nearly all endeavors, large and small, can benefit from having a *vision*. If we are taking on a new client, we need to know the client's vision for success. When thinking about our life in the future, we need to envision the ideal day-to-day life. A certain intellectual rigor and honesty applied to deeply understanding either our personal or professional hopes will allow us to articulate a vision we and others can act on. A vision should be concise, clear to all and recognizable when achieved.

Once a vision is clearly established it can be brought to life. I trust my *instincts* over my mind in making many decisions, but that wasn't always the case. Pablo Picasso once said, "Computers are useless. They can only give you answers." Our minds, like computers, can also be too rational. Our intuition takes in a richer perspective and can guide us to a new way of seeing. Developing the ability to listen to my instincts has taken years, and it has happened by learning to quiet my mind. I believe instincts hold a deeper knowledge that can be more useful in finding a better way. Unique creativity, for example, often comes from learning to tap into subtle nuances of feelings formed outside the reaches of the mind's rational thought processes.

But nothing happens in the world until our instincts move us to take *action* toward our vision. The old adage "Nothing succeeds like success" is misleading. The truth is, nothing succeeds like hard work. To really understand the action component of VIA, we need to embrace good old-fashioned hard work. I got excellent advice from one of my first bosses. "Coleman," he said, "you will never be the smartest person in the room, but you can always be the hardest working." Hard work can be deeply gratifying and is almost always seen from those who are finding ways to unleash new kinds of growth in the world. If you want to evolve and bring about change, be prepared to get your hands dirty.

A good example of how we brought Vision, Instinct and Action together to help a client find a better way was when CBS RADIO (then called Infinity Broadcasting) hired us to help turn around year-over-year sales declines brought on by the onslaught of the digital music revolution, which was in full swing with no clear end in sight. A return to the old days of radio's dominance was unrealistic; the organization had gotten too comfortable depending on the same formula that had worked for many years. The best hope was a new vision. We studied the landscape, competitors and consumers carefully. What became clear was that Infinity had to commit to constant reinvention. As a medium, radio is current and nimble, and has broad reach. We needed to take those attributes and challenge the company and the whole industry to see how hard they could push the medium.

The new vision was for Infinity to become the most flexible online/offline platform in advertising. The campaign we created captured that vision in one line: "How Far Will You Go?" The answer: "Infinity." The company kicked off a massive effort to move all stations online. Advertisers started designing innovative national programs to experiment with new online/offline models. Using our instincts, we created one of the most emotional and powerful campaigns we had ever developed. We went all out to put it into action. We challenged ourselves to see how far we would go in the advertising. We wanted to use an iconic photograph of Jamaican reggae musician Bob Marley in the campaign, but his estate told us they never used his image for commercial purposes. We kept working on the proposal, making the case that radio had been the primary medium for getting Bob Marley's message out to the world.

When we went further by offering to make a donation to fund the return of his body to Africa for final burial, they reconsidered. That's going pretty far to find a better way. And the company's sales grew for the first time in years.

Act Like You Believe

There are no shortcuts to any place worth going.
—*Beverly Sills*

If we're trying to do something authentic we will develop certain behaviors that demonstrate our commitment to our beliefs. Like they say, "If you can't walk the walk, don't talk the talk." It's often difficult to stick to those defining behaviors, but that's what makes them so important. Remaining true to our principles takes discipline, but the rewards are liberating when we do. Since every company is different, the pillars that define our beliefs will vary. Here are a few behaviors we adhere to that make VIA, VIA:

Take time to live

I've always respected people who work hard during the day and get out the door with enough time in the evening to do the things they love. People who get their work done and leave whenever they want are applauded at VIA, not made to feel guilty because they don't spend every waking hour at work. As a matter of fact, we have unlimited vacation. People take off as much time as they need, as long as they get their work done and it's coordinated with their teammates. I believe it's critical to have a rich life outside of work; it allows people to come to work full of energy, ideas and enthusiasm. That's why it's vital for people to take vacations, and why we reward people who've worked 10 years or more at VIA with the opportunity to take a sabbatical to reflect, recharge and sometimes even reinvent themselves. If we don't have time to build meaningful relationships with family and friends, we'll wake up one day without any.

Profits get shared
VIA believes that if we work hard and the company prospers, everyone should benefit. So we've always had a profit-sharing bonus plan that includes everyone in the company. The money is important, but it has just as much to do with respect. We always say that everyone at the agency matters; every single person contributes to our collective success. Not sharing the profits we achieve together would contradict this core belief. When people are recognized for their contributions, they are much more likely to feel respected and valued.

Everyone is an owner
When I was 12, I went on an epic trip to Ireland with my godfather, Steve Fitzgerald. In the middle of the trip we got lost on some back road, and when he tried to turn around, the car got stuck in a ditch. Well, this turned into my first driving lesson, in a car with a standard transmission no less. He pushed, I ground the gears and the car slowly, painfully scraped up over the edge of the road. I turned around to see him shrug and say, "That's why we rent, John. That's why we rent." It's the truth. We always seem to take better care of the things we own. We get a sense of pride from ownership, and in return, we give the things we own a special level of care. That's one important reason why VIA is an employee-owned company.

We all create
I think few things in life feel as good as having the opportunity to develop and share our creativity. Not only is creativity the core of our business; it's one of the most important human needs. At VIA, we know good ideas can come from anyone. And they need to come

from everyone if we are going to be the best we can be. So cultivating a culture of contribution from all corners of the agency is both great for our company and clients, and deeply enriching for everyone in the company. In my opinion, every organization needs, at minimum, some kind of suggestion box coupled with an open-door policy—not just any open-door policy, but a wide-open-door policy so that all ideas find a way to be shared.

Give back until it hurts a little
Doing pro bono work is as important for the agency as any work for paying clients. If we believe there's more to life than just money, anything we can do to help lift up the people and organizations where we live will make for a better existence for us all. So in the spirit of it being better to give than receive, we will always want to put our creativity and passion to work for causes we believe make the world a better place.

So these are a few ways we behave that actualize VIA's principles. It's critical for every group to have its own principles and behavioral expectations—if they don't exist for your group, then you have your first task starting tomorrow: Make them clear and real. But they are useless if we aren't disciplined enough to live by them.

I've worked with VIA Group Client Strategy Director Julia Brady for years. She is extremely disciplined about taking care of herself, maintaining her diet and exercise regimen no matter what. On a typical business trip with a pack of VIAns, we'd all be wolfing down burgers, fries and beers after a long day, but she'd quietly pull out a container of salad and water from her bag, unknowingly making the rest of us feel like savages. If she weren't so nice she'd be incredibly annoying. I once asked her why it was so easy for her to stick to her healthy ways. "Practice," she said. In 1990, Julia decided she was going to compete in the 1992 Barcelona Olympics in solo sailing. Though a sailor, she had never raced in that style of boat, and two years is a short time to master such a craft. That made her a huge underdog. But she plotted out a nearly day-by-day regimen for those two years of training and ended up winning a bronze medal in the event, a remarkable feat. But the biggest takeaway was the lesson she learned that the more you commit to the behaviors you know are right, the easier it is to believe anything is possible.

Pragmatic Optimism

Great things are done by a series of small things brought together.
—*Vincent Van Gogh*

Some people see the glass as half empty; some see it as half full. I say, "Let's drink." It's so hard in this world to put forth new ideas, to drive new thinking and real change. It takes much less energy to say, "That won't work." Or, "We've done that before and it failed." Or, "What's wrong with keeping things the way they are?" Maintaining the status quo is easy. Saying no, even easier. Being negative is the lazy way. It takes energy and commitment to put forth "new." Answers to most complex challenges require much work, openness and inventiveness to realize. So how can change happen? Through pragmatic optimism.

President Abraham Lincoln was a pragmatic optimist. He believed all people should be treated equally. But he knew he had to attack the problem bit by bit to bring all the naysayers along one step at a time. Martha Graham, whose influence on modern dance has been likened to Pablo Picasso's on visual arts—for setting out to reinvent modern movement in a male-dominated field—was a pragmatic optimist. Each small step she created changed the way of seeing the beauty in new movements. People who want to usher in change need to keep one eye on the prize and one eye on the crowd. If we lose the crowd, we could lose the prize. If we lose sight of the prize, we could melt into the mass of inaction embodied by the crowd. Pragmatism ensures that our energy will be well-spent and well-directed. But optimism provides the inspiration to continue even when our energy dwindles to a trickle.

Being an optimist isn't simply living with rose-colored glasses on. It's a very practical technique for staying focused and inspiring others around us to stay on task. Being pragmatic while remaining optimistic ensures that our visions are realized. One without the other can create problems. If obstacles are not assessed honestly, being too optimistic can erode credibility, while being too pragmatic can result in cautious and uninspired efforts that fail for lack of risk taking.

A few thoughts if you tend to err on the side of optimism:

- Set goals that are a stretch but objectives that are achievable.
- Don't fake or lie to cover up a bad situation. Just tell the objective truth; no one can stand being told a load of crap.
- Do your homework; the more prepared you are, the more likely you will be successful, because you will fully understand the situation.
- Cry more (it will make you feel better; constant optimism is a fake existence).

A few thoughts if you tend to err on the side of pessimism:

- When confronting negative events, acknowledge all your emotions, good and bad, but focus your attention on the things you can control to improve the situation.
- When communicating with others, share encouraging and supportive advice; ranting rarely helps.
- Being a little more impulsive may lead you to try more new things.
- Laugh more (it's never as serious as you think).

In late 1999, the first internet economy was booming. VIA was coming off two years on the Inc. 500's list of fastest-growing companies. My gut told me to raise some outside capital, the company's first—partly because I thought the internet boom might never stop and we should invest more capital to maximize growth, and partly because I had an intuitive feeling that the internet explosion was a little too good to be true. I did raise some money, closing the funding in January of 2000, on the optimistic outlook that the internet trend was not going to slow down. And then—pop! The internet bubble burst officially on March 10, 2000. Everything unraveled, and fast. Without that capital infusion I don't think VIA would have made it through the downturn. That's pragmatic optimism in action. Or maybe just blind luck. Either way, VIA lived to fight another day. I think it was, and always has been, due to the blend of pragmatism and optimism that has guided the place.

Dream an Impossible Dream

A dream you dream alone is only a dream.
A dream you dream together is reality.
—*Yoko Ono and John Lennon*

We inhabit this planet for the blink of an eye. Too often we forget that fact. What makes human beings special is our free will to create—to make things, do things, be things that are only defined by our dreams. The problem comes when we forget to dream. I am positive that a life chasing an impossible dream is better than one with no dreams at all. And really, any dream works. Our dreams can be small. I just think we need them.

That's where belief comes into play. Believing in ourselves and our dreams gives us confidence and hope that seem to provide some level of happiness. Dreams, however, are rarely achieved alone. We often need to work with all different kinds of people—glad, sad, mad and even bad—to achieve them. To chase after impossible dreams, we need everyone pulling in the same direction. It's not enough to just believe in yourself. We need to believe in the people around us too. I remember when Group Client Strategy Director Dan Bailin, who bleeds VIA red, first asked to present the introduction of the agency at one of our pitches. As CEO, that was normally my job, but I believed he was ready to do it. Though a little nervous, he got up and started explaining what VIA was about and why it was so special. In the middle of his pitch he got all choked up. Now, like in baseball, there is no crying in advertising. But in this case it worked; the new client understood that someone who cared so much about his own agency would make for a great believer in his business and brand. Years later that client called Dan the best account person he'd ever worked with. That's the benefit of believing in the people around you; it motivates them to greatness.

Like the American novelist Ernest Hemingway said, "The best way to find out if you can trust somebody is to trust them." Well it's the same with belief. When we start conveying our belief in the people around us, we'll see astonishing things. They'll do things they've never tried before. They'll open up to new ideas. They'll start supporting each other in amazing ways, and bonds will form that can lead to unstoppable teamwork. An email sent by former Project Manager Kelly Scharf to a VIA team upon completing an epic yearlong internet project makes that point. She congratulated the large, diverse group on their heroics and shared the motto the team had developed to get them through the challenges: One Heartbeat. This motto, apart from showing their flair for the dramatic, also illustrated that because they believed in each other so much they started acting as one, which led them to achieve the near impossible. Ta-da. Believing in each other really works.

Nothing great ever happens until someone starts believing, even when it doesn't make sense. The hardest leadership period I ever survived came at the end of 2001. We had barely navigated the internet bubble downturn when the events surrounding 9/11 forced us to close our New York office. We lost many clients as work dried up, and we shrunk to less than half our size, but at least we had one anchor client we could count on, a big semiconductor company. We were planning on doing a multimillion-dollar web assignment with them that had been in the works for months. With that assignment I could keep the company going. We had a Monday morning meeting scheduled to kick things off. I was standing with my team in the client's lobby when the leader approached me to ask for a word in private. He told me the project was likely being canceled, delayed at best. The budget had dried up. And with it, my hopes for holding VIA together vanished.

I decided not to tell my team right then. Instead, I said there had been a delay. We all went out to lunch, and everyone was laughing and shooting the breeze. I was the only one who knew how dire the situation was, and I kept a calm exterior in spite of my wheels racing inside. It was a sickening feeling. Would I lose the business? Would I lose my house? How would I tell everyone? Fun stuff. That afternoon I had a prospecting sales call at a regional financial institution called Banknorth. I didn't feel like going at all, but I decided to keep the introductory meeting that I had been trying to get with the head of technology for months, even though it seemed like a distraction against the backdrop of the morning's news.

As I sat down in her office, she began telling me that earlier that very morning Banknorth's CEO had appeared on CNBC television and committed to Wall Street that Banknorth would have internet banking set up within a couple of months. However, there was no initiative in place to do that. Fortune favors the bold, I thought. Although VIA had never done an online banking site, and at that time had almost zero business-to-consumer marketing experience, I got up to her whiteboard and started diagramming a potential solution for her like a person possessed. In the end, I remember making some sweeping analogy between online banking and a grand piano. Lord only knows why. But I left that meeting with a new million-dollar assignment—that we delivered on in spades—and Banknorth became our most critical client for the rest of the decade. Most importantly, I learned to never stop believing.

If there is one thing the VIA experiment continues to teach me, it's that the world and the people in it never, ever fail to surprise me. So against all odds, we've got to believe. When we do, we are rewarded with the most amazing of journeys.

A Few Final Thoughts About Principles

In a gentle way, you can shake the world.
—Mahatma Gandhi

The prevailing economic model of capitalism many people live under has numerous variants; it can be blamed for much hardship and many ills in the world, while it can also be credited with advancements and the elimination of much suffering. If the principles that guide the leaders of corporations and governments are grounded in greed, fear, insecurity and indifference, then capitalism has grave effects. However, when leaders and companies adhere to principles grounded in creativity, collaboration, caring and compassion, I believe capitalism can help create tremendous positive change and new growth while working toward minimizing the harmful effects that too often result from its existence.

So perhaps it is time to reimagine and evolve capitalism. The simplest and most dramatic way to do this is by challenging those operating within the capitalist systems to make decisions and take actions guided by principles that embody hope to bring about this new kind of growth. The ideas and experiences I chose to share in this book illuminate principles that I believe can lead organizations to greater collaboration, compassion and collective creativity. But in my opinion, an organization can only truly be its best if the individuals within are happy and fulfilled. However, organizations can only do so much to help their people reach their potential. We all have to take responsibility for seizing our opportunities and creating our own happiness in life. So I recommend actively cultivating personal principles. It can take years to unlock the principles that will best guide our own lives, but for me, nothing has been more important.

Without silver bullets or big shortcuts in this process, we all have to find our own answers. And because we're all different—with unique stories, backgrounds and needs—I doubt that any two people will wind up with the same guiding principles. They will most likely evolve over time as we each gain new insights from our personal growth. Some of our principles might come from our religious beliefs or mentors; others we may discover on our own. But the simple act of contemplating these principles can bring great clarity to daily living. Here are a few principles I try to live by:

Be Present
It seems so simple, but if I practice staying present—that is, not spending time regretting things in my past or worrying about my future—almost always I immediately feel peaceful. Being aware in every given moment, without judgment, leads to my greatest contentment and helps me see clearly how I might respond to whatever situation I find myself in.

Want for Nothing

There was a time when I was too driven by money and accomplishment, probably from a sense of insecurity, so this principle might be interpreted to mean "acquire as much wealth and stuff as you can." Actually, however, I mean just the opposite. The older I get, the more I understand that to live simply is to be free. I actively try to let go of perceived wants and desires every day, and when I do, I am more content. To want for *absolutely* nothing would then mean *complete* contentment. At the end of the day my wife and I usually take a moment to recount a few things for which we are grateful; this simple act of appreciating what we have instead of longing for what we don't have seems to make us both a bit happier.

Take Good Care

Some people take *great* care with everything. For me, that approach leads to excessive caution, exhaustion and usually disappointment from unachieved expectations. But a lot of people take *lousy* care of almost everything, and that's a recipe for disaster. So I aim for taking *good* care—of my body, my family, my relationships, my business, my community, my dog, our environment. It is never as simple as I think it should be, but I try. As Oscar Wilde said, "Everything in moderation, including moderation."

Kindness Doesn't Hurt

My philosophy for being in the world is simple: be kind. It's not always easy though. When someone attacks me or my beliefs, I often switch into fight or flight mode instinctively. However, I try to stay open, accept those around me and remember that we are all doing the best we can. If we could all drop the "eye for an eye" mentality and remember to "turn the other cheek," this simple shift might save the world from destroying itself. Or we could try to behave with Buddha's centuries-old wisdom in mind: "Silence the angry person with love. Silence the ill-natured person with kindness. Silence the miser with generosity. Silence the liar with truth."

Make Better

I am happiest when I am creating. Being drawn to the new thing that lives just beyond my hands, mind or heart is the wellspring of my energy. But I try to remain mindful about having the acts or art I put into the world be in service of others, not solely for my own benefit or pleasure.

Under our generation's watch, digital technology has transformed nearly every aspect of our lives: finance, health care, transportation, energy, agriculture and entertainment. Yet sadly, the world today seems filled with more hatred, violence, mistrust and repression than ever, and the great potential for technology seems lost when it fuels those maladies. Perhaps what we need now is a revolution of our principles. A revolution to find ways of being more civil. More respectful. More caring. And more effective at using the wonders of our age to help eradicate war and repression, ignorance and poverty, sickness and suffering.

It's a tall order, but creating a dialogue around the importance of shared principles is a good place to start, and it can begin with you. So start talking about principles that matter—to you, your family, your community, your company and your government. Make a big deal about forcing the conversation. Try to uncover principles that could make a difference in our world. But most importantly, start living up to your own principles. The example you set could spark a peaceful revolution toward a better world for all.

VIA PRINCIPLES
Finding Growth Through Creativity, Collaboration and Compassion

Reflection and Discussion Guidelines

... it is proposed that a form of free dialogue may well be one of the most effective ways of investigating the crisis which faces society, and indeed the whole of human nature and consciousness today. Moreover, it may turn out that such a form of free exchange of ideas and information is of fundamental relevance for transforming culture and freeing it of destructive misinformation, so that creativity can be liberated."
—David Bohm

This portion of the book is filled with questions divided into sections matching the book. Some questions are meant for personal reflection, and some are meant to help foster dialogue in the groups you may belong to. (I use the word *group* here, but it could mean *company, community, organization, team, family,* etc. Pick the term that best applies to your situation.) I believe this book will be much more valuable to you if you spend time exploring these questions and make the effort to bring some of what you discover into your daily life.

Don't be shy or overly formal about starting a meaningful dialogue in your group. It can happen over a business lunch, a family dinner or a scheduled event. I have conducted hundreds of group discussions, and 90 percent of the time participants are enlivened by the interactions, often sharing that they wish they had more meaningful and substantive conversations in life. There are many good resources online for helping you structure different discussion and dialogue groups. But if you are armed with a handful of good questions and a willingness to ensure that everyone is contributing—and you can model deep listening yourself—you will create rich opportunities for dialogue that leads to valuable growth. The important thing is to take the initiative to spark the critical conversations our communities need to have.

Introduction:
In Search of a New Kind of Growth
(Refer to Pages xi-xiv)

Personal Reflection:

1. What principles do you believe in today? Do you live by them? Why or why not?

2. What does growth mean to you? What kind of growth do you want from life? What would your ideal future look like? How do you handle change?

3. What does wealth mean to you? Would you adapt your principles to attain it? Is it really better to give than receive? Why?

Group Dialogue:

1. What is a principle? How should principles be determined and used by individuals and groups?

2. How would you describe your group's current guiding principles? Are there others you would like to adopt? If so, what are they? Do you live by them? Why or why not?

3. What does growth mean to your group? Is it based on more than just money? What are all the dimensions of growth your group could create? How could your group serve your community, shareholders, executives, employees, customers and surrounding environment?

As a result of this investigation, what new opportunities do you see? What new principles could you cultivate? What new ideas have you created? And what actions could you take?

Be Curious
(Refer to Pages 5-14)

Personal Reflection:

1. How are you cultivating and expanding your understanding of the world? When was the last time you truly challenged yourself to seek out an alternative point of view? Have you pushed yourself to grow enough?

2. What activities excite you or stimulate your level of energy? How can you find ways to fill your life with more activities like those?

3. What have you thought about learning to do for years? Why haven't you? Who taught you something today?

Group Dialogue:

1. What is your group's purpose? Is it clear to all? If not, try to reach a better understanding of the collective purpose. Is it meaningful? What are your group's unspoken aspirations?

2. How are new ideas brought to life in your group? How does your group embrace and enable change? How do members share new ideas and information? Can this be improved?

3. How do fear and the status quo weigh on your organization or group? Is challenging the status quo encouraged or discouraged? What can the group do to more pervasively make change and share new knowledge?

As a result of this investigation, what new opportunities do you see? What new principles could you cultivate? What new ideas have you created? And what actions could you take?

Honor the Process
(Refer to Pages 15-24)

Personal Reflection:

1. Do you follow a process in undertaking important pursuits? Describe it and think about how you could improve it.

2. What is the most successful way for people of different backgrounds, beliefs, motivations, power or privilege to communicate with each other? Do you believe in good and bad conflict? How do you get groups of people to understand each other or work together?

3. Do you control your life, or does your life control you? Do you take initiative or let others take the lead? Is this good or bad?

Group Dialogue:

1. What are your vision, mission and core beliefs? What value do they add to the world? Do they do any harm?

2. What does your group do well together? What prevents your group from working better together? How could you strengthen the way your group collaborates?

3. Does your group have a clear decision-making process? How does your group work through challenging situations?

4. Is your group afraid of failure, conflict, sharing or risk taking? Where does resistance to change come from, and how can you eliminate it? Is your group open to learning from failure? Do you go out of your way to make sure all voices are heard?

As a result of this investigation, what new opportunities do you see? What new principles could you cultivate? What new ideas have you created? And what actions could you take?

Think Like the Audience
(Refer to Pages 25-35)

Personal Reflection:

1. Do you tend to listen or speak more—how are your skills as a speaker and a listener? When listening to someone, are you fully attentive?

2. What value do you get from having diverse people, thoughts and experiences in your life? What role does this diversity play when you're creating your best possible work?

3. What causes matter to you and why? Do you feel obligated to give back to society somehow? If so, are you doing enough, too much or too little? Do you live your life with compassion? How can you gain more compassion for those around you?

Group Dialogue:

1. Does your group deeply and thoroughly understand the people it serves? Is everyone in the group heard? How could the group garner deeper understanding of the communities it serves?

2. Describe your best learning experience. Why was it so effective? Is your group diverse, and how does that benefit or affect the way the group operates? What existing barriers limit diversity, and how could they be eliminated?

3. Explore whether caring more about your efforts matters or not. What could greater empathy with people connected to your group teach you? How does your group show compassion? Does it matter?

As a result of this investigation, what new opportunities do you see? What new principles could you cultivate? What new ideas have you created? And what actions could you take?

CREATE RESPECT
(Refer to Pages 37-48)

Personal Reflection:

1. Who are some of the people you deeply respect in life? Why? How can you adopt some of their traits?

2. Do you set a good example for creating positive interactions in your life? How could you foster more respect in the communities you are part of? Are you tolerant and accepting of people different from you?

3. What causes are you willing to make a true personal sacrifice for? What does it mean to be a respected citizen in your community? Would you be willing to do more? Are you willing to take the necessary steps to make it happen?

Group Dialogue:

1. What is your group's reputation? Do you garner respect in your community? How is the perception of your group different from who your group really is?

2. What does integrity mean to your group? How important is integrity to your group's success?

3. Are people in your group treated with respect? What changes would you like to make to your group's culture, and how could you bring them to life?

4. How is respect built in your group? Who are the most respected people in your group? What are some of the issues your group is most willing to fight for?

As a result of this investigation, what new opportunities do you see? What new principles could you cultivate? What new ideas have you created? And what actions could you take?

BE ON TIME
(Refer to Pages 49-61)

Personal Reflection:

1. What moments in life bring you the most joy? What changes or commitments could you make to increase the amount of time you have for such moments and activities?
2. When someone asks you how you are, do you often say very busy? Is that good or bad? How do you prioritize your life: Time with friends and family? Work? Time for yourself?
3. Are you organized or loose? Are you early, prompt or late? Are you dependable or inconsistent? Are you happy with how you use your time?

Group Dialogue:

1. How could your group demonstrate greater initiative, speed and agility? How does your group use or waste time? Do meetings start and end on time? Are they too long? Too big? Productive? How could they be improved?
2. How does your group deal with crises, deadlines and bottlenecks? Is free time worked in for open play, thinking and new exploration? Why or why not?
3. How does your group keep pace with the state of affairs in the markets, your communities and the world in general? Is your group current enough to create connections and new ideas?
4. How does your group bring in new people? Is there a culture compatibility assessment? Is that good or bad? Does the group invite enough people with constructive differences? How could the group's dynamics be constantly assessed and improved?

As a result of this investigation, what new opportunities do you see? What new principles could you cultivate? What new ideas have you created? And what actions could you take?

BE ON BUDGET
(Refer to Pages 63-70)

Personal Reflection:

1. Do you live to work or work to live? What does having enough money mean for you?
2. What does it mean to be fair in your financial dealings? What does being greedy mean? What can money buy and not buy?
3. Does money make you feel secure? Successful? Happy? Worried? Why?

Group Dialogue:

1. How could your group increase profits? Does your group invest money in the right things? Where is money wasted, and where could money be saved? In what new ways could your group make money? What would a dramatic return on investment look like for your clients or your group?
2. Does your group deal with money in an open, transparent and fair way? Why or why not? How are money and its distribution handled? Is your group generous enough? What is the ownership structure of your company, and does that benefit the correct parties fairly?
3. How do the links between money and society affect your group now? Is it OK that wealth is becoming more concentrated, or should that change? Are taxes a good investment in making society better, or should taxes be lower to allow capitalism to determine wealth distribution?
4. Is globalism good or bad? What's the best way to provide the greatest care for all people, and what would you change to improve people's lives if your group had all the power in the world? Try to avoid typical political narratives (e.g., more/less government) and focus instead on innovative ways to improve society for all.

As a result of this investigation, what new opportunities do you see? What new principles could you cultivate? What new ideas have you created? And what actions could you take?

Figure It Out
(Refer to Pages 71-82)

Personal Reflection:

1. Have you given up on anything you wish you hadn't? What have you thought about tackling but never tried? Do you think you're persistent? Why or why not? How do you maintain enthusiasm and energy to achieve goals? Is it working?

2. Are you self-reliant? Do you carve out enough time for yourself or too little? Why? What gets you stuck?

3. When was the last time you tried something that made you nervous or scared you? Should you push yourself more?

4. List everything that worries you; then imagine how your life would be different or the same if all your problems were solved. What is your biggest problem today? Try to plot three new ways to approach solving it—is one worth trying?

Group Dialogue:

1. What are the most interesting ways your group has solved problems? What traits make your group excellent at problem-solving? When does your group get stuck? List your group's biggest obstacles and analyze why they are not getting resolved. Where does the group find motivation? What affects morale? Is your group collaborative enough? Why or why not? How could you improve problem-solving?

2. How open is your group to new ideas, data, practices and people? Is change easy? How does your group discuss and resolve problems? What traps and barriers burden the group? What groups do you admire for their innovation? What could you learn and adopt from them?

3. How does your group handle failure? Is it resilient? Does your group shake itself up periodically? What five new things might lead to more energetic innovation? What are the best ideas you have seen this year? How could you take one and weave it into your group's work?

As a result of this investigation, what new opportunities do you see? What new principles could you cultivate? What new ideas have you created? And what actions could you take?

FIND THE MAGIC
(Refer to Pages 83-98)

Personal Reflection:

1. How important to you is creativity, as a creator or a consumer of others' creativity? Do you make a practice of creating things you're interested in? If so, could you strengthen your practice? If not, why? What keeps you from being as creative as possible?

2. Do you play enough? Do you have friends or relationships that encourage you to explore new ideas, experiences and endeavors? What ideas scare or excite you? Have you tried a new creative activity in the last year? Why or why not?

3. What is your favorite work of art? Book? Movie? Music? Dance? Building? Product? TV show? Why? What do you get from the art you experience—think broadly about the definition of "art." Do you care what people say about your work? Why or why not?

Group Dialogue:

1. Is your group's environment inspiring? Is there passion or love for the work your group does? If not, how could the work, environment or interactions become more interesting and invigorating? Is enthusiasm part of your culture? What excites people in your group? Do play and exploration enter into your group's activities?

2. List the three most inventive, innovative or creative things your group has done. How did they come about? Does anything stifle creativity in your culture? Are members encouraged to collaborate and share ideas? Why or why not? How effective is the sharing of criticism and feedback? What are the most creative things your group admires in the world? How could those things inspire your group's process?

3. What single innovation could your group benefit from creating? How might you make it real?
4. How would your group apply the word *beauty* to describe what you do? Do resources always trump the group's effort to do things for the sake of their magic or beauty?

As a result of this investigation, what new opportunities do you see? What new principles could you cultivate? What new ideas have you created? And what actions could you take?

Do Work That Makes You Proud
(Refer to Pages 99-108)

Personal Reflection:

1. What work are you most proud of? Why? Is pride constructive or distracting? How do you think about your work—is it a reflection of *who* you are or simply a necessity?

2. Do you like taking credit for your work, or are you quick to give it away? Is that good or bad? How do you set standards for your work? Are they so high they keep you from trying new things or so low that you never feel challenged?

3. Do those around you value your contributions? Do you feel fairly compensated for your work and its quality and value? Have you thought about starting a business? What would it be, and how might you do it?

4. What one contribution might you make to the world?

Group Dialogue:

1. Define doing your best. How does quality apply to your group's effort? What is your group most proud of? Does your culture encourage improving or expanding understanding?

2. How is success shared? How is failure handled? What is cause for celebration? What are the best ways to celebrate your group's endeavors? Is recognition consistent? Should there be more or less? Is pride constructive or destructive for your group?

3. Do you think your group has high aspirations or sets its sights too low? Why? What embarrasses your group? How do you challenge each other to grow?

4. How could your group create more positive impact in the world? Does your group fairly share the rewards and value created?

As a result of this investigation, what new opportunities do you see? What new principles could you cultivate? What new ideas have you created? And what actions could you take?

BELIEVE
(Refer to Pages 109-121)

Personal Reflection:

1. What values do you believe in deeply? Which have proven helpful? Which have not? Do you embody your values? Would others agree? Why or why not?

2. Are you living the life you hoped for? What happens when something you believe in conflicts with others in your life?

3. How do you balance giving back to your community and focusing on your own needs? Are you disciplined about maintaining health? Happiness? Obligations?

4. What does living a good life mean? Are you too optimistic? Too pessimistic? Why? What are your dreams for yourself and your children, family, friends and the world? What would you risk to make them happen? What does real happiness look like?

Group Dialogue:

1. What does your group believe in deeply? An early principle at Google was "Don't be evil." How does that apply to your group's goals and initiatives? What is your group's worth?

2. Are there clear behavioral expectations for group members? Is your group generous? Why or why not? What happens when someone's actions are out of character or harm the group? If the leaders don't follow the group's principles, can they be challenged?

3. Does your group dream? How does your group set expectations and goals? Does leaving a legacy mean something? Will the future be brighter or darker? How will your story read at the end of life? Write it now.

4. If your group had a motto, what would it be?

As a result of this investigation, what new opportunities do you see? What new principles could you cultivate? What new ideas have you created? And what actions could you take?

A Few Final Thoughts About Principles
(Refer to Pages 123-126)

Personal Reflection and Group Dialogue:

1. How could you create greater fairness, safety, wellness, kindness, sustainability, joy or awareness in the world?

2. Would you choose to help many people a little or a few people a lot? How responsible should current generations be to future ones? How locally should we operate in a digitally connected world?

3. If technology continues to mechanize certain kinds of human work, can the current economy find new ways to support people's lives? How do you prioritize your work, pleasures and values?

4. Are people becoming more polarized in their views and beliefs? If so, how can they be brought together in this kind of environment?

5. Write up to five simple statements that express your personal guiding principles.

As a result of this investigation, what new opportunities do you see? What new principles could you cultivate? What new ideas have you created? And what actions could you take?

Acknowledgments

I would like to deeply thank my family—Linda, Erin, Hannah and Samuel—whose support in writing this book was invaluable and whose love has made my life so rich. And my parents, Jacquelyn and Richard Coleman, for their constant inspiration.

I would also like to thank those who helped review this book before its first publishing: Greg Smith, David Burfeind, Leeann Leahy, Ivan Salazar, Jessica Fidalgo, Bill Burke and Mark Nakell.

A huge thank-you goes to Patti Lanigan for her amazing editing talents. Thanks to Chris Cote for his gifted design skills and to Marissa Henry, Perdy Mullins, Duane Holmblad and Jenn Arredondo for helping coordinate this book's production.

And of course, this book would not have been possible without the stellar work all the employees of VIA do every day.

About the Author

John Coleman is the Chairman of The VIA Agency, a marketing and advertising shop he founded in 1993 in Portland, Maine. Coleman holds a B.S. in mechanical engineering, an MBA and an honorary doctorate in fine arts from Maine College of Art. He sits on the board of trustees for the Skowhegan School of Painting & Sculpture and is a volunteer for the Preble Street Resource Center. Coleman enjoys fly-fishing, yoga and playing the guitar, and maintains an active studio practice exploring conceptual artwork. He and his wife, Linda, live in Maine, where they grew up and raised their three children.

He can be contacted at jcoleman@theviaagency.com.

I believe our principles are part of us, known to us deep down, even if they are not clearly identifiable or easily articulated. To explore this idea, I spent 10 minutes reflecting on each of VIA's principles and painting my creative expression of its meaning. This action-painting method with no breaks between canvases gave me no time to think. The paintings on the opposite page are what came out in the work and what I believe. The cover of this book is a composite of these images.

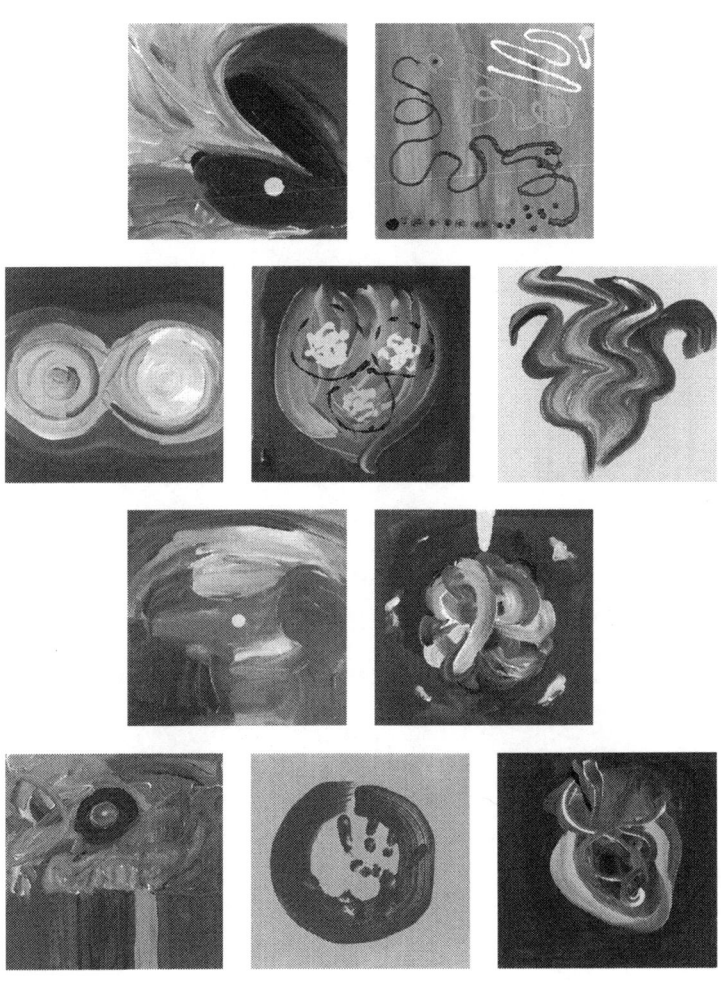

Principles
September 17, 2014, 10:11–11:51 a.m.
Paintings by the author
Acrylic on canvas, 16 × 16 in.

Colophon

The book design and page layout for *VIA PRINCIPLES* were inspired by medieval incunabula using the golden canon of page construction by J.A. van de Graaf, as popularized by Jan Tschichold. The type is set solely in Minion Pro composed with Adobe® InDesign® Creative Cloud®. The symbol used throughout the book is based on a golden spiral: a logarithmic spiral whose growth factor is 1.618 ... , or the golden ratio. The 10 circles correspond to the 10 principles.

Made in the USA
Middletown, DE
03 April 2017